Critical Reflections about Students with Special Needs

Stories from the Classroom

Jennifer J. Coots, Editor

California State University, Long Beach

Kristin Stout, Editor

California State University, Long Beach

PEARSON

Boston • New York • San Francisco
Mexico City • Montreal • Toronto • London • Madrid • Munich • Paris
Hong Kong • Singapore • Tokyo • Cape Town • Sydney

Executive Editor: Virginia Lanigan
Editorial Assistant: Matthew Buchholz
Senior Marketing Manager: Kris Ellis-Levy
Production Editor: Janet Domingo
Editorial Production Service: Publishers' Design and Production Services, Inc.
Composition Buyer: Linda Cox
Manufacturing Buyer: Linda Morris
Electronic Composition: Publishers' Design and Production Services, Inc.
Cover Administrator: Joel Gendron

CEC Standards quoted throughout this book are from What Every Special Educator Must Know: The International Standards for the Preparation and Certification of Special Education Teachers, Fifth Edition. Copyright © 2003 by the Council for Exceptional Children.

For related titles and support materials, visit our online catalog at www.ablongman.com.

Between the time website information is gathered and then published, it is not unusual for some sites to have closed. Also, the transcription of URLs can result in typographical errors. The publisher would appreciate notification where these errors occur so that they may be corrected in subsequent editions.

Library of Congress Cataloging-in-Publication Data

Coots, Jennifer J.
    Critical reflections about students with special needs / Jennifer J. Coots, Kristin Stout.
        p. cm.
    Includes bibliographical references.
    ISBN 0-205-49606-7
    1. Children with disabilities—Education. 2. Special education. 3. Reflective teaching.
I. Stout, Kristin, 1972– II. Title.
    LC4015.C66 2006
    371.9—dc22

                                                                            2006049837

Printed in the United States of America

10 9 8 7 6 5 4 3 2 1   11 10 09 08 07 06

Contents

CHAPTER 4

Individual Learning Differences   29

CHAPTER 5

Instructional Strategies   39

CHAPTER 6

Learning Environments and Social Interactions   51

CHAPTER 7

Language   61

CHAPTER 8

Instructional Planning   73

CHAPTER 9

Assessment   82

CHAPTER 10

Professional and Ethical Practices 92

CHAPTER 11

Collaboration 103

About the Editors

Jennifer J. Coots, Ph.D., is the coordinator of the Master of Science in Special Education program at California State University, Long Beach. She learned about the need for effective problem-solving skills as a classroom teacher and teacher trainer. As director of a longitudinal research project, she learned about the power of qualitative methods. This book brings together those areas of interest.

Kristin Stout, M.S., draws from her 10 years of experience as a classroom teacher in both general education and special education to currently teach courses for the Education Specialist Credential program at California State University, Long Beach. As a private consultant, she works closely with families and schools to support students in inclusive placements.

Contributors

Kelly Carter-Skillman is a special education teacher and is pursuing her M.S. in Special Education at California State University, Long Beach.

Rebecca L. Dennis, M.S., formerly a middle school special education teacher, now teaches at California State University, Long Beach.

Joy Dye, M.S., has been teaching students with special needs since 1994 and mentors beginning-year teachers.

Jolie Foster-Berman, M.S., is a special education support teacher.

Jennifer Kagy, M.S., is a special educator at an elementary school.

Amy Larsen, M.S., formerly an elementary special educator, now lectures part time at California State University, Long Beach.

Robert J. Markel, M.S., is a middle school special education teacher.

Kim Martin, M.S., is a special education teacher at the elementary level and also lectures for California State University, Long Beach.

Cayce Saunders, M.S., teaches a special education program at an elementary magnet school.

Glenna Stewart, M.S., is an elementary special education resource teacher.

Joyce Su, M.S.,is a special education resource teacher who works with elementary-aged students in both a general and special education setting.

Kimberly Ufholtz, M.S., an elementary-level special education teacher, also teaches in an adult educational program.

Angie Villani is a special education resource teacher at the elementary level.

Acknowledgments

This book began over breakfast. A group of graduates from the Special Education Credential Program at California State University, Long Beach ate together and shared stories about problems they were facing in their classrooms. The group was the Demonstration Teacher Network from California State University, Long Beach. This collection of outstanding graduates demonstrated skills in the area of critical reflection as they shared stories with each other and sought guidance or just a shoulder to lean on. The group decided to formalize the sharing of these stories by putting them into written vignettes, with the idea that perhaps these stories could be of use in helping other teachers develop their skills in the area of critical reflection. After presenting the vignettes at a conference, the group was urged by conference participants to make these vignettes available by seeking to publish them.

Our thanks therefore go to all members of the Demonstration Teacher Network from California State University, Long Beach; those conference participants who gave us encouragement for this project; and to the people at Allyn and Bacon, particularly Yvette Angel and Virginia Lanigan, who have helped bring this project to its conclusion.

Additionally we thank our reviewers: Joe M. Blackbourn, University of Mississippi; Elizabeth Cramer, Florida International University College of Education; Sarah M. Ginsberg, Eastern Michigan University; and Jack Hourcade, Boise State University.

We also thank our families for their help along the way. How could we have dealt with the pressure of deadlines, cats walking on keyboards, or children refusing to take naps without their support? We also gratefully acknowledge the children with disabilities and their families who have motivated us to continually develop our knowledge and share that information with others. You are our inspiration.

CHAPTER ONE

Introduction

*G*ood teachers are good problem solvers. They are faced with a unique set of learners in each classroom and must apply what they know about the content they are teaching and what they know about teaching strategies to this unique set of learners. This role involves teachers in problem solving to arrive at many decisions during each school day as they balance these factors. Good problem solving requires critical reflection as teachers customize what they have learned about content and teaching strategies to the unique needs and abilities of their students. The benefits of systematic critical reflection, according to Reagan, Case, and Brubacher (2000), are that reflective practice

- "helps free teachers from impulsive, routine behavior";
- "allows teachers to act in a deliberate, intentional manner"; and
- "distinguishes teachers as educated human beings because it is one hallmark of intelligent action" (p. 26).

The process of customizing knowledge through critical reflection involves a process of interpretation. Teachers must develop local meaning in order to change their practices to align them with what is described in the literature on effective teaching. As noted by Riehl (2000), "Real organizational change occurs not simply when technical changes in structure and process are undertaken, but when persons inside and outside of the school construct new understandings of what that change means" (p. 60). The construction of new understandings can present complex challenges for teachers as they examine their current practices and learn how to incorporate new changes. As such, good teaching becomes a life-long learning process. Wilson and Berne (1999) state that such "learning, real learning is hard work. You read, you think, you talk. You get something wrong, you don't understand something, you try it again. Sometimes you hit a wall in your thinking, sometimes it is just too frustrating. Yes, learning can be fun and inspiring but along the way, it usually makes us miserable" (p. 200).

The vignettes presented here are not always examples of learning that makes teachers miserable, but they are good examples of how teachers sometimes get things wrong and need to try again as they apply new things they learn. They are not always examples of best practices, but they are good examples of how real teachers have constructed local knowledge of effective practices. We emphasize that these are real stories from real teachers about real children and real schools.

The teachers in the vignettes have all engaged in reflective practice. York-Barr, Sommers, Ghere, and Montie (2001) describe the characteristics of reflective practitioners as including being "committed to continuous improvement in practice," assuming "responsibility for his/her learning," demonstrating "awareness of self, other, and the surrounding context," developing "thinking skills for effective inquiry," and taking "action that aligns with the new understandings" (p. 10). They also state that critical reflection can be fostered through journaling, observing, engaging in dialogue, and examining case studies. In case studies, the complexities, realities, and joys of teaching are presented in narrative form to accentuate problems to be solved (York-Barr et al., 2001). Grenot-Scheyer, Fisher, and Staub (2001) state that the use of case studies or vignettes can be pivotal to the problem-solving process. Through reconstruction and interpretation of an event in a written vignette, one can organize thoughts and present information in a systematic way. This helps in the problem-solving process and can lead to successful action to resolve the problem. Reading, discussing, and developing case studies represent one way in which reflective teachers can "learn systematic ways of reflecting on their own practice so that they can enhance their students likelihood to succeed" (Eby, Herrell, & Hicks, 2002, p. 7).

Although critical reflection can take on many forms such as meditating, praying, listening to music, or even sharing horror stories (Reagan et al., 2000; York-Barr et al., 2001), more systematic reflection such as developing case studies or vignettes may be more effective in turning thoughts into action (Eby et al., 2002; Reagan et al., 2000). Reagan and colleagues (2000) share the story of a new teacher, Amy, who engaged in active, deliberate reflection and critical analysis. Her systematic reflections served as a guide for future action and were therefore proactive in nature. Systematic critical reflection and action should go hand in hand.

We prepared these vignettes so that teachers and those training to be teachers can experience the problem-solving situations that some others have faced as they engaged in reflective practice, making a connection between their students, their content knowledge, and their knowledge of effective teaching. We hope, first, that these vignettes will introduce teachers and future teachers to the types of problem solving involved in teaching. We also hope that these vignettes will introduce teachers and future teachers to the power of vignettes to spark effective problem solving and systematic critical reflection. Then, maybe our readers will begin to write their own vignettes about their own experiences and truly be reflective practitioners.

Here is what one of our graduates and contributors, Joy Dye, shared about the power of reflective practice in her own beginning years as a teacher.

While thinking through and compiling case studies, I was reminded of my first two years of teaching. I was completely in basic survival mode. There was so much to learn and so many new responsibilities put upon me, I had to learn fast. This didn't leave much time for personal reflection. I worked during the day and went to school at night. One thing that really helped me was having a trusted guide. Joan was an experienced and respected teacher who took me under her wings and showed me that I can be the teacher I always wanted to be.

After the first year of teaching, I thought I wasn't quite sure if I would continue teaching. After the second year, I felt more sure of myself and had a much stronger foundation in which I could begin to develop my teaching craft. It wasn't until the third year of teaching that I became a reflective teacher. By then, I knew for sure that I wanted to be a teacher. I knew in my mind that I wanted to be a teacher that could change the lives of the students, give them the skills necessary to achieve their goals. I wanted to be the best teacher I could possibly be.

Writing these case studies reminded me of where I was in my personal journey the time these different situations occurred. Each of the case students I wrote were learning experiences for me. I was reminded of what I read in Henderson's (2001) book on reflective teaching. He shared the perspectives of a teacher who said that she sees frustrations not as obstacles, but as hurdles. She said, "Obstacles will stop you but hurdles move you forward." Through reflective teaching, I have evolved and continue to evolve into the teacher I desire to be. I have experienced frustrations and hurdles, but I have grown and learned from them.

Council for Exceptional Children Standards

Teaching students with exceptional needs can present particular challenges for teachers but also opportunities for critical reflection as teachers work to meet the unique learning needs and abilities of these students. Whether the students have been given labels of learning disabilities, autism, visual impairments, or the many other labels that would make a child eligible to receive special education services, teachers are charged with developing and implementing individualized educational programs. The process of individualizing is in and of itself a problem-solving situation, and, as such, can be assisted by developing skills of critical reflection. The opportunity to confront and resolve real problems faced by real teachers, as presented in these vignettes, can give teachers practice in using skills needed for critical reflection to meet the needs of students with exceptional needs. We therefore wrote these vignettes to assist teachers in developing skills of critical reflection across important areas in special education whether they are general education teachers or special education teachers.

We have grouped the vignettes according to the Council for Exceptional Children's 10 professional knowledge and skill standards for special education. The Council for Exceptional Children (CEC) is the largest professional organization of special educators and has a history of advocating for well-prepared, high-quality teachers for students with exceptional needs. These standards provide guidance for effective teachers of children with exceptional needs across the following 10 areas:

1. Foundations
2. Development and Characteristics of Learners
3. Individual Learning Differences
4. Instructional Strategies
5. Learning Environments and Social Interactions
6. Language
7. Instructional Planning
8. Assessment
9. Professional and Ethical Practices
10. Collaboration

We have focused on the core standards and presented just a few sample standards at the start of each chapter. All the common core standards are presented in Appendix A. We also direct the reader to review CEC's standards for specific credentialing areas. These specific areas are:

Mild/moderate disabilities	Physical and health disabilities
Severe/profound disabilities	Visual impairments
Deafness and hearing impairments	Early childhood
Emotional and behavioral disorders	Diagnosticians
Gifts and talents	Administrators
Learning disabilities	Technology specialists
Mental retardation/developmental disabilities	Transition specialists

After each vignette, we have included a set of questions to guide reflections on these standards as they can inform decisions about situations in a classroom. The coding following each question refers the reader to the CEC Common Standards. For example, (CC3K1) stands for **Common Core** area **3, Knowledge** Standard **1:** Effects an exceptional condition(s) can have on an individual's life. These vignettes are assigned to specific categories and questions are derived from those, but most of the vignettes address issues that cross multiple categories. New questions can therefore be expanded beyond the specific chapter within which each vignette is found. A cross-reference of all vignettes by other standards is found in Appendix B to help with this process.

The first vignettes in each chapter are the most basic in nature. These basic vignettes present challenges that can be solved with introductory knowledge of special education. Throughout each chapter will be a mix of vignettes with some relying on introductory knowledge of special education and some relying on more advanced knowledge to engage in effective problem solving. We hope that these vignettes as a whole will assist teachers in developing the critical reflection skills that are essential as they work to apply generalized knowledge about special education to their own particular students and school site.

CHAPTER TWO

Foundations

$\mathcal{T}$he vignettes in this chapter reflect CEC Standard 1 related to the historical, legal, social, political, and economic foundations for the delivery of special education services. They also reflect some of the struggles teachers face as they implement educational practices in alignment with state and district mandates. As such, the vignettes help to elucidate the craft involved in developing programs that fit the intent of the law as well as the letter of the law. Interpretation of the mandates of the Individuals with Disabilities Education Act, including providing a Free and Appropriate Education (FAPE), education in the Least Restrictive Environment (LRE), Due Process, and Non-discriminatory Assessment can be difficult, as these vignettes will demonstrate.

Selected CEC Common Core Standards: #1 Foundations

CC1K1   Models, theories, and philosophies that form the basis for special education practice

CC1K3   Relationship of special education to the organization and function of educational agencies

CC1K4   Rights and responsibilities of students, parents, teachers, and other professionals, and schools related to exceptional learning needs

CC1K8   Historical points of view and contribution of culturally diverse groups

CC1S1   Articulation of personal philosophy of special education

What Do I Believe?
....

Hansford sat down and began to write an outline for his paper. He had been asked by his university instructor to write down his personal philosophy of education. He wasn't sure where to begin. He remembered reading a paper in which teachers who had a good reputation for teaching diverse groups of students, including students with disabilities, had shared their personal philosophies. One of the things they said was that they believed in helping each child learn to do his or her personal best. They believed their classrooms were communities and that every child should have access to the core curriculum. Hansford remembered being especially intrigued by the teacher who said:

> *I believe every child can succeed. That doesn't mean that we can think of our version of what success is and that every child is going to reach that. But I think that every child can have success and become a valued citizen. And every child deserves that access, that equal access to a curriculum that the school offers on a grade level. Because I believe that they all deserve that opportunity and they all can succeed. (Coots, Bishop, & Grenot-Scheyer, 1998, p. 326)*

Hansford also believes that every child can succeed, so he knew that was an important part of his philosophy. He went on to complete this assignment and identify the other things that he believed about education. He wondered, however, how he would be able to put that philosophy into practice. Would he really be able to help every child succeed?

QUESTIONS FOR REFLECTION
....

1. What is your personal philosophy of education? (CC1S1)
2. How will you translate your philosophy into practice? What challenges do you think you will face? (CC1S1)

The Silent Parents

....

BY KIM UFHOLTZ

Ms. Wash teaches at an elementary school located in a low socioeconomic area and most of the parents are not proficient in English. Her students are culturally diverse and learning English as a second language. Parent participation at the school is generally minimal. During most IEP meetings and student conferences, a translator facilitates the communication between teachers and the parent. All too often, the parents are silent partners in this decision-making process. Ms. Wash doesn't know if this is due to a lack of parental education, a language barrier, not knowing their rights, or a lack of concern. Ms. Wash wants to change this, but isn't sure where to begin.

For one of her university courses she was taking to earn her master's degree, Ms. Wash had read about the concept of "personalismo," which she understood to mean making personal connections with families. She had read that for many families, this personal connection was what was most important and she wondered how personal the connection was at the IEP meetings. Everything seemed so formal and legalistic, with forms to be signed and reports to be read. How could she apply this notion of "personalismo" in her dealings with parents at IEP meetings and on an ongoing basis? She also had been reading that for some families, teachers are so highly respected that it would be a sign of great disrespect for a parent to "speak up" to a teacher at a meeting. How could she deal with this? She wanted the parents of her students to "speak up" but if their culture didn't value this, should she push this issue?

QUESTIONS FOR REFLECTION

....

1. What are some of other cultural and linguistic factors that might lead families to be "silent partners" with the school staff? What suggestions do you have for Ms. Wash to make more personal connections with the families of her students? (CC1K7, CC1K8)
2. What are the cultural and historical factors that might be contributing to the formal nature of the IEP meetings that Ms. Wash has experienced? (CC1K9)

Too Many Boys

Mr. Kim's caseload was getting full. As a special education resource teacher at the elementary level, he usually averaged 28 students. When Mr. Kim reflected on the students in his caseload, it was hard to miss the fact that 75 percent of them were boys, all identified with learning disabilities. Mr. Kim often wondered why there were so many boys with learning disabilities in this community.

Today, he was preparing for an initial IEP for a fifth-grade student named Marquis. The school psychologist had already submitted his report and it clearly showed that Marquis qualified for special education services based on a diagnosed learning disability. Mr. Kim had spent considerable time with Marquis over the last months, both pulling him out of the general education class and observing him in the general education class, and although convinced that this student required extra assistance and attention, he wasn't convinced that Marquis had a true learning disability. Mr. Kim was basing this opinion on his own experiences in working with students with disabilities. But he recognized that it was just that—an opinion.

Although Mr. Kim had a high level of regard for the school psychologist, he wasn't convinced that Marquis's "learning disability" wasn't actually a "classroom disability." Mr. Kim had observed the challenges the fifth-grade classroom teacher faced in getting Marquis to attempt any work. He noted the frustration evident in the teacher's body language whenever they held a conference about this student. Marquis seemed to be constantly confused in class, as he had difficulty paying attention to what the teacher was saying. He was constantly getting up out of his seat, talking with neighbors, and playing at his desk. He could never seem to complete even a portion of the assignments given. It seemed that Marquis was constantly in trouble—due in part to his own actions and in part to the teacher's frustration level. Mr. Kim also noted the way Marquis seemed to snap to attention and begin working whenever he was receiving one-on-one attention from the male aides who shared a similar cultural background to him and when he was in an environment that wasn't distracting.

QUESTIONS FOR REFLECTION

1. What type of information should Mr. Kim collect to help him support this opinion that Marquis isn't a student with a disability? (CC1K4)
2. How might the school structure and cultural factors be contributing to so many boys being identified as having a learning disability? (CC1K9, CC1K10)
3. How does Mr. Kim resolve the issue of providing services to boys who really require special education support while not contributing to their overidentification? (CC1K10)

Ms. Petrie had been honored when the principal had asked her to serve as co-chair of their school's task force on educating all students in the least restrictive environment (LRE). She knew that their school district had been taken to court because of the large number of students still educated at special education centers. The district had a much higher percentage of students educated at such centers than the national averages and also the highest percentages in the state. She also knew this was a complex issue and would take a lot of teamwork to bring the district into compliance with the LRE mandates. She also knew that the principal had asked her to serve on this task force because of the many discussions they had had about possible changes that could happen at her school. The principal seemed pleased with the information Ms. Petrie was able to share from the readings she had become familiar with during her credential work. She also knew that the other teachers had elected her as a "grade-level chair" because they respected her problem-solving abilities. All of this contributed to her feeling honored and prepared to face the task at hand, but she admitted that she was scared because the task seemed so awesome!

The principal and the co-chairs decided that one of their first steps should be to hold a parent meeting. They knew a lot of rumors were swirling around and they wanted to reassure the families and answer whatever questions they might have. They asked all the teachers to personally inform their students' parents about this meeting and to explain the purpose so that hopefully there would be a large turnout. They also arranged to have refreshments served and provide child care.

On the night of the meeting, the principal and co-chairs were happy to see a lot of parents in attendance. They knew not everyone was there but they felt that a good cross-section of families were there. Ms. Petrie looked around and saw many faces she recognized from her many years of teaching at the school and thought that familiarity might help. The meeting opened with just a few brief comments about the court case that had led to this discussion. The families were told that nothing had been decided about what would happen for their school but that the hope was more of the students at the district's schools would have the opportunity to be educated alongside their nondisabled peers. Ms. Petrie gave a brief overview about the benefits of children with disabilities being educated alongside their nondisabled peers and then asked the families to share their hopes and fears about this possibility. Many parents raised their hands to speak. The first speakers said they didn't want their children to leave the center. One father said that his child had been educated at a "regular" school when he was in first and second grade and had been teased and no one seemed to know how to best educate his child. Another mother said that she felt comfortable at the center. Her child had been attending the center for five years and so the family felt they know the teachers and staff. Another father said that he wanted his child to stay at the center because he felt the center staff cared for and protected his child. The parents spoke for over an hour, with the theme of protection being most frequently mentioned. The families felt that their children were more protected at a special center than they would be at a "regular" education site. When they were nearing the time that they had said the meeting would end, Ms. Petrie and the other school staff said they would end the meeting as planned but would schedule another meeting to talk with the families soon.

Ms. Petrie, her co-chair, and the principal decided to meet for a short while after the meeting to debrief. They were pleased by how open the parents were in sharing their concerns. People clearly held strong feelings but, overall, were able to keep their emotions in check. Ms. Petrie praised the principal for how well he had reassured the parents when their emotions started to swell. All in all, they agreed it had been a good meeting. Ms. Petrie, however, was even more concerned now about their next steps. She agreed that the district had not done enough in the past to provide opportunities for the students at their center to be educated in the LRE. How would they ever be able to convince the parents that their children would be safe and well educated once they left the center?

$\mathcal{Q}$UESTIONS FOR REFLECTION

1. How might Ms. Petrie and her task force members respond to the parents' concerns? (CC1K7)
2. What are some of the supports that could be put in place at the regular education sites to alleviate parents' concerns? (CC1K6)
3. What broader systems change elements should be addressed in this situation? (CC1K1)

Dr. Banks had just finished meeting with his graduate students who were all special education teachers and was surprised by what he had heard. They were feeling under attack by all the different things they were being asked to do. Their districts seemed to be regularly mandating new practices, saying these things were required by No Child Left Behind or IDEIA. The teachers said these practices didn't seem to agree with each other. For example, they were being given standardized, packaged curricula because the district said that the teachers needed to use these "research-based approaches." They said they didn't think the research was always that good. Dr. Banks's students stated that it was hard to individualize these packaged curricula and that they lamented not being able to use programs that they had found to be effective in the past. They were being required to use publications with prewritten IEP objectives for improved accountability but believed that these limited their ability to reflect individual needs on students' IEPs. Some teachers remarked that with all the testing now required for accountability, their students were being pushed aside since they took an alternate test that "didn't count" in accountability reports. Some teachers also noted that they were being told by their district that they were no longer considered "highly qualified" even though they had been rated highly by their principals. They felt their professionalism was being challenged. Dr. Banks had worked with this group of graduate students for a few years and was truly surprised by the level of frustration they were expressing. They had always been vocal about the challenges they faced in their daily teaching but they had also demonstrated good problem-solving skills. He wondered what he could do to help these students deal with these new frustrations.

QUESTIONS FOR REFLECTION

1. What suggestions can you share with these teachers as they deal with these systemic responses to educational mandates? (CC1K3)
2. What can teachers do when they feel that they are being asked to engage in practices that don't fit with their views about the theories and philosophies that form the basis for special education practice? (CC1K1)

To Evaluate or Not?

Lolo arrived in the United States three years ago. Having come from the Pacific Islands, living in multiple locations with multiple dialects, he had yet to develop a dominant use of any one language. He began attending school in the United States in second grade, and now in fourth grade, his situation was creating some great challenges for the staff at Ridgemont Elementary. One challenge was that Lolo was big for his age and felt it necessary to use his size to pick on anyone who gave him what he thought was negative attention. He sometimes tried to intimidate teachers and other staff members.

The school psychologist had been carefully following Lolo's progress and knew some important information about his background that led him to be leery of starting a special education evaluation. Mr. Hamblin, Lolo's fourth-grade teacher, couldn't understand why he *wouldn't* be evaluated. Didn't Lolo display all the signs of a special education student: performing at a kindergarten academic level and showing limited grasp of the English language? And what about his behavior? The teacher thought surely that Lolo was emotionally disturbed as well, since he had never observed the kind of behaviors seen in Lolo in his many years of teaching.

During Lolo's early years of development he never had the opportunity to receive any type of formal education. Additionally, Lolo was never able to grasp the different dialects of the regions in which he and his family lived. His siblings didn't display these similar delays because they were given the opportunity to attend school. Lolo spent his early days working alongside his father.

The school psychologist at Ridgemont Elementary felt as though he couldn't honestly say that Lolo's delays in language acquisition and academic achievements were not a result of his limited exposure to school and environmental factors. How could he identify Lolo as a special education student until these factors had been ruled out?

*Q*UESTIONS FOR REFLECTION

1. How can the team at Lolo's school site ensure that due process issues are addressed in his case and that a special education referral is necessary? What factors should be considered? (CC1K6, CC1K5)
2. What academic and behavioral supports should be put into place to help Lolo immediately if he is found eligible for special education? What if he isn't found to be eligible? (CC1K4, CC1K2)

Ready or Not. . .

BY AMY LARSEN

"I just don't feel Brian is ready for inclusion yet," said Mr. Wright of his eighth-grade student. "Brian is a leader in my class and I depend on him to help other students. He is just beginning to gain confidence in his abilities and I think he will lose that if he leaves this self-contained special education class. Besides, I don't think he wants to leave. Brian gets plenty of mainstreaming during passing periods and lunch."

Brian's parents weren't sure how to respond. They remembered the earlier experiences Brian had had with inclusion. It had not gone well. They had been reading about inclusive models since that time and realized that it had not gone well because Brian had not had the services that would have helped him do well.

Brian also wasn't sure how he felt about an inclusive placement. He remembered how, in elementary school, he had felt lost most of the time. He felt different and like he didn't really belong. He also remembered being teased when he couldn't keep up with the other kids. He liked his current special education class placement because he didn't feel different and he could help the other kids. They also did a lot of fun things in his class and he doesn't remember having that much fun in his general education classes.

QUESTIONS FOR REFLECTION

1. How can the team work together to resolve the differences of opinion about the best placement for Brian? What strategies can be used to help resolve differences of opinion between parents and their children? (CCIK7)

2. What are the cultural and historical factors that might have contributed to Brian's feeling different and being teased by other kids when he was in elementary school? (CC1K8, CCIK9)

Resource or Self-Contained Class

BY ANGELA VILLANI

Josephine is a third-grader in a literacy-focused class. She has a twin sister and both of them are loving and enjoyable to be around outside of the classroom. Josephine and her identical twin have been learning English at our school since kindergarten. As toddlers they had spoken Spanish with their family, but they frequently used words of their own to communicate with each other.

You know it's Josephine you're watching as you walk through the school building because she's the one dancing the length of the hallway, whereas her identical twin follows the class in line. Josephine loves to tell long detailed stories about her pets and movies that she's seen. She draws with the skill and speed of a cartoonist, explaining the metamorphosis of a butterfly in accurate and colorful pictures.

But Josephine doesn't like school. She told me that very matter of factly. She says she wants to play on the playground or color or go home, where she can play. She doesn't like to sit at a desk; she'd rather stand to write. At shared reading on the rug, she sits in the back so she will have room to scooch around and wiggle a bit. Josephine still sometimes goes back to her old habits of licking her fingers and picking up things off the floor and tasting them. Josephine likes to sit with her resource teacher one to one and read stories, especially those with lots of pictures. She will tell her teacher all about the action in the pictures, using complex sentences, but she sometimes struggles with the English vocabulary and asks her teacher if she understands the Spanish word she says. Josephine doesn't like to work on phonics. She doesn't like to work on sight words either. But she can sound words out, and she will practice sight words if her teacher makes a competitive game out of it. She can write fanciful one-paragraph stories on a topic of her choice with just a few grammatical errors if she gets a lot of encouragement to keep working and some help with spelling. And Josephine doesn't like to practice her math facts unless she is working toward a reward.

Josephine, who doesn't like to take tests, performed poorly for the school psychologist when she was tested for special education support. She passed the end-of-first-grade reading benchmark in second grade, but has not yet passed any reading test for her third-grade general education teacher. Much of her school day is spent avoiding tasks that she does not want to do. Her identical twin sister performs a little bit better, and encourages Josephine to follow the rules (which irritates Josephine). Her low scores, her performance on assigned tasks in the classroom, and her behavior caused many on her IEP team to think that Josephine belonged in a self-contained special education class. The resource teacher argued for the general education placement with continuing pull-in resource help and additional supports, saying Josephine shows her intelligence through art, stories, and dancing when she has a choice, but is not always motivated to perform academically.

1. How might cultural factors be influencing the situation here and how might such factors contribute to the overrepresentation of culturally/linguistically diverse students in more restrictive placements? (CC1K5)
2. What potential difference in values, language, or customs at home might exist between home and school? (CC1K10)

Retention and Social Promotion

BY GLENNA STEWART

Prior to scheduling an IEP meeting for Henry Tatupu, the special education teacher scheduled a meeting with the general education teacher in order to determine Henry's progress in the general education curriculum. Henry is considered an "English language learner" who is receiving special education services for a specific learning disability.

During the meeting, the general education teacher related that she was concerned about Henry's lack of progress in the general education curriculum and his failure to meet grade-level standards. Ethically, she felt she could not promote Henry to the next grade level. She had already undertaken steps to retain Henry for the next school year. She had prepared an academic intervention plan, which recommended retaining Henry. Mr. Tatupu said that the teacher knew best, so he and his wife would agree to retain Henry.

This information took the special education teacher by surprise. She felt, intuitively, that it was unethical to retain a student who was receiving special education services. She believed that retaining a student with an individualized education program was a clear violation of the principles of IDEIA. She wondered what she might be able to do at this point to influence the decision that had been made to retain Henry. She began to reflect on her practice, and how she might advocate for change in the paradigm of retaining and social promotion.

QUESTIONS FOR REFLECTION

1. Do the principles of free and appropriate education and least restrictive environment run contrary to the practice of retaining students receiving special services? If so, how does the practice of retaining students violate the two principles? (CC1K1)
2. Do you agree with the special educator that it is unethical to promote students who have failed to meet grade-level standards? Why or why not? (CC1K3)
3. How might the cultural differences between the parents and the school personnel have influenced the action of the general educator? (CC1K10)
4. What cultural and historical factors underlie the practices of retention and social promotion? (CC1K1, CC1K8)

Baby Steps

BY KIM UFHOLTZ

Leslie's first year

Leslie is beginning the first grade at a new school with her teacher, Mrs. Hall, in a self-contained special education class. Leslie has cerebral palsy and requires a good deal of physical support for most activities. Her primary language is Spanish but she states her wants and needs adequately in English. Leslie has made tremendous progress since birth because intervention began when she was an infant and she has been in a school setting since the age of 3.

On the first day of school, Mrs. Hall had not been informed that she would be having a student who used a wheelchair, therefore she was not prepared. She knew immediately there would need to be accommodations made in the room so that Leslie could have access to core curricular activities. Also, Mrs. Hall felt a little uncomfortable because she was not sure she could provide the necessary support to Leslie and provide adequate instruction to the other students in her classroom. Mrs. Hall did have one classroom aide in the morning to help her and that was some relief, but no information had been provided to explain how to provide the supports Leslie would require for personal care issues, transferring to a chair or desk, eating, and so forth. There was no adapted equipment provided. Mrs. Hall was in a portable classroom with two doors but one door had stairs to exit. The bathroom was not accessible for a wheelchair. Mrs. Hall was filled with questions. Where was Leslie's IEP and file? Why wasn't information provided to Mrs. Hall prior to the first day of school so she could have been prepared? Who was going to come and help her learn to provide the appropriate physical supports?

QUESTIONS FOR REFLECTION

1. What first steps should Mrs. Hall take to plan for the unique physical supports Leslie will require? (CC1K4)
2. How should the school district have handled Leslie's transition into Mrs. Hall's class differently? (CC1K6)

Leslie's second year

After the first year, all of Leslie's supports are in place. She has special equipment to use in the classroom and the playground and for her personal care, and she has an aide who "shadows" her to meet her physical needs. Leslie is a happy girl and loves to participate in whole-group and small-group instruction. As Leslie has made tremendous progress in academic areas and loves to socialize with her classmates, Mrs. Hall feels that Leslie should be spending more time in a general education classroom.

Mrs. Hall decides to call an IEP meeting to discuss this possibility, but when the parent arrives, she is adamant that Leslie should stay all day in Mrs. Hall's class. She is concerned for Leslie's safety and feels her physical needs would make her unable to participate adequately in the new setting. The general education teacher speaks and tries to eliminate Mrs. Hall's fears and even invites Leslie's mom to visit her classroom. A second meeting is scheduled to discuss the topic again after her mom has a chance to visit the classroom. At the second meeting, Leslie's mom still insists that Leslie will not benefit from being in the general education classroom. Mrs. Hall feels very frustrated because she wonders why a parent would not want her child to be included in a general education classroom with the opportunity for interacting with her nondisabled peers. Since there is a translator at the meeting, she wonders if language barriers are getting in the way. She also wonders how cultural and personal beliefs might be influencing Leslie's mom's decision.

QUESTIONS FOR REFLECTION

1. How can Mrs. Hall effectively convey to Leslie's mom the benefits of a least restrictive environment? (CC1K10)
2. What other kinds of preparatory activities could Mrs. Hall have engaged in prior to the IEP meeting? (CC1K1)
3. What should Mrs. Hall do now to give Leslie a chance to participate in an inclusive setting as she believes Leslie would benefit from this greatly? (CC1K6)

Leslie's third year

Mrs. Hall and her students have moved to a new school. Last year, Mrs. Hall overcame some issues with integrating her students by developing a relationship with another general education teacher. She had her entire class included in the general education classroom for some academic instruction and she had been making plans to further increase these opportunities. She still thinks Leslie should be educated in a general education classroom. Leslie's mom is still not happy about the issue but Mrs. Hall feels she is starting to come around. She seems to feel reassured because Mrs. Hall understands her concerns and puts Leslie's safety first.

Leslie's mother is now concerned, however, because Leslie's aide is not feeding her at lunch. Since Leslie is 8 years old and can maneuver a fork and spoon in her right hand, Mrs. Hall felt it was important for Leslie to start building some independence and had allowed her to begin feeding herself. Leslie's mom is also unhappy because Leslie isn't achieving at the same pace as her sister. Mrs. Hall tries to reassure the mom that Leslie has made tremendous gains in all areas and mentions the general education classroom issue again. She tells Leslie's mother that this might help Leslie make even more progress.

At their next meeting, Leslie's mom says she has decided to let Leslie spend time in the third-grade classroom. Mrs. Hall is thrilled! Leslie is happy, too. Leslie's aide goes with her into the general education classroom. Things are going well and Leslie is thriving. She is developing new friendships outside the special education classroom. At recess, the new friends are socializing and playing together. The new challenge for Leslie and her team, however, is safety on the playground. Leslie uses her gait trainer at recess most often and her aide stays close by her, but it is sometimes difficult for Leslie to participate in the group's activities.

QUESTIONS FOR REFLECTION

1. What factors do you think contributed to Leslie's mom's new decision about integration? (CC1K6)
2. What should Mrs. Hall do to improve the partnership she is developing with Leslie's mom and try to find some compromise that will help the team work together to meet Leslie's individual needs academically, socially, and in daily living skills? (CC1K7)

Development and Characteristics of Learners

*T*he vignettes in this chapter reflect CEC Standard 2 as they provide examples of how teachers appreciate the unique characteristics of each of their students. They also show how effective teachers understand typical trends in development as well as the range of individual differences that can be found in students receiving special education services and those who do not receive those services. In addition, the vignettes reflect how effective teachers understand how developmental issues impact the ways in which teachers teach the whole child and interact with his or her family.

Selected CEC Common Core Standards: #2 Development and Characteristics of Learners

CC2K1   Typical and atypical human growth and development

CC2K2   Educational implications of characteristics of various exceptionalities

CC2K3   Characteristics and effects of the cultural and environmental milieu of the individual with exceptional learning needs and the family

CC2K5   Similarities and differences of individuals with and without exceptional learning needs

CC2K7   Effects of various medications on individuals with exceptional learning needs

Surgery Will Make It All Better

BY REBECCA DENNIS

Quentin is a student with cerebral palsy. Although he requires a wheelchair for long distances, he can walk around the classroom without assistance. He uses assistive technology for writing due to spasticity in his arms and hands.

At his annual IEP, Quentin's teacher reviewed his present levels of performance. She explained that Quentin was two grade levels below where he should be in reading but he was doing a great job in all of his classes and working really hard. After that she asked if there were any questions from the parents. At this point in the meeting they questioned, "Do you think that if Quentin has surgery, he will become normal?" Confused by the question, his teacher shot a look to the school nurse and asked the parents to explain. They went on to clarify that they believed Quentin's disability to be a physical one that surgery would heal and then he would be normal. They said their church community had even begun praying for Quentin's recovery after surgery, as they too believed he would be healed.

Quentin's teacher wasn't sure how to respond to this. She wanted to be respectful of the parents' beliefs but she didn't believe that surgery would make Quentin "normal." He experienced a whole set of learning problems. She did think that surgery would help him in a lot of ways but she didn't think that was what the parents meant.

*Q*UESTIONS FOR REFLECTION

1. Quentin's parents believe that he will be like "typical" children after surgery but his teacher disagrees. Is it important to distinguish between ways in which Quentin is "typical" and "atypical" in his development? Why or why not? (CC2K1)
2. How should the team respond to the parents' impression that Quentin's condition is one that surgery will "cure"? How can the professionals demonstrate respect for the cultural/religious views of these parents if they disagree with what the family has said? (CC2K3)

22

....

CHAPTER 3

*Development
and
Characteristics
of Learners*

The "Monster" in My Classroom

....

BY JOYCE SU

The phrase "one mistake can ruin your life" is never truer than in the world of education. One curse word, one month of not turning in your homework, one unfortunate incident, and a child can be labeled a "bad" student. She will get talked about in staff lounges and have a code name that every teacher in the school knows. So, naturally, when Ms. Dumas received the IEP of a certain student from another district in the first month of her first year of teaching, she freaked out.

On paper, this student, Mandy, sounded like a nightmare. On top of being labeled with a learning disability, she had a couple other labels tacked on—the kind that made a teacher go "whoa." By the time she finished reading the IEP, Ms. Dumas found herself dreading the day this little girl would walk through the door.

The next day, Mrs. Dumas ran into Mandy's future teacher, Monica. From the teacher's reaction to the mention of Mandy's name, she could tell that Monica also had the same fears about this new student. Both of them were dreading the incoming "monster" of a student. They spent their time together attempting to encourage one another and develop an initial plan of action for needed support.

Later, when she entered Monica's classroom, Mrs. Dumas was immediately introduced to Mandy, a sweet-looking girl in pigtails. After their first meeting together, she was able to determine that Mandy was an entirely different girl in person than on paper. Sure, she struggled with academics. Yes, she had attention problems. But the outrageous behaviors that she had read about didn't seem to be present. Even after the initial adjustment period, Mandy continued to behave in a manner totally contradictory to what was mentioned in the IEP.

The experience showed Ms. Dumas the importance of not judging a student by what she read. She thought it was discouraging that other professionals might have the same initial reaction to Mandy as she did. The initial information received about a student can be highly persuasive in determining attitudes toward them.

QUESTIONS FOR REFLECTION

....

1. Given the vast differences between individuals with disabilities, how can teachers minimize preconceived ideas about students? How might stereotypes and preconceived ideas impact the things that teachers do? (CC2K6)
2. How can teachers write accurate reports about students that help teachers have positive first impressions of them and their similarities and differences from other students with and without disabilities? (CC2K5, CC2K6)

What a Label Changes

Ms. Montel is worried about her student James. The initial IEP meeting has just been set, and Ms. Montel is dreading this meeting. You see, James has just been identified as a student who exhibits "autistic-like" behaviors. His parents returned with this diagnosis after a number of extensive doctor visits, based on a referral generated from the school psychologist's assessment. Ms. Montel is concerned about one of her students having this label. What changes will it cause? Will it change the way the students interact with James? Will it change the ways she teaches James? How are his parents handling this information that can seem so life-changing? Will she be able to provide the level of support and modifications that he needs? What does he need?

The classroom was quickly becoming inundated with specialists and it is all a bit overwhelming. Someone wants to work on James's speech, another specialist wants to take him out of the room to give him occupational therapy, and now a resource teacher from special education is talking to her about team-teaching techniques. It seems like too much! Wasn't it easier when Ms. Montel thought of James as a really challenging student but a challenge she was willing to take on? Now with this label of autism, Ms. Montel feels uncertain that she has received the training she needs to work with James. How will she work effectively with all these people?

QUESTIONS FOR REFLECTION

1. What would you say to Ms. Montel to alleviate her concerns? (CC2K2)
2. How does this case study show some of the dangers inherent in having services based on labels? Is there a danger in using labels that emphasize differences rather than similarities? (CC2K5)

Elmo

BY REBECCA DENNIS

Mrs. Marley has been working as a teacher of students with moderate to severe disabilities within an elementary setting for the past three years. Recently, she made a transition to a middle school. She has spent her first year within the middle school brainstorming ways to teach the students and keep them interested while providing age-appropriate materials. However, it has been a struggle, as some of the parents of her students still seemed to encourage them to watch television shows such as *Sesame Street* and play with stuffed animals. Trying to maintain a healthy balance, Mrs. Marley worked with the parents by introducing more age-appropriate materials.

One day, a parent phoned to ask if Mrs. Marley would mind having a small birthday party for her son near the end of the school day. Without hesitation, Mrs. Marley agreed. As the birthday party started, the student's mother showed up with a person dressed like Elmo, the student's favorite character from *Sesame Street*. Not knowing how to handle the situation, Mrs. Marley allowed Elmo to entertain the students during the party but noticed that the other middle schoolers rolled their eyes and snickered.

QUESTIONS FOR REFLECTION

1. How should Mrs. Marley address the atypical development of students, balancing this with age-appropriate materials? (CC2K1)
2. What, if anything, could Mrs. Marley have done differently in this situation, playing special attention to culture/characteristics of the family? (CC2K3)

Should He Graduate?

Ara's family left his IEP feeling very confused. They had told the staff that they wouldn't need an interpreter at the meeting because they were feeling confident about their abilities to understand English, their second language. Now they wondered if they should have had one present at the meeting. The staff had asked them whether they had planned for Ara to graduate from high school with a diploma and they had responded enthusiastically, "Of course!" The staff at the IEP meeting then started to talk to them about all sorts of things like certificates of completion, exit exams, and transition planning—all new terms to the family. Ultimately, the staff seemed to be saying that they didn't think Ara could graduate with a diploma. Ara's parents felt shocked by this news. When the meeting ended, Ara's parents felt like they were in a fog. They hadn't really understood much of what was said at the meeting and weren't sure what the final decision had been at the meeting. Ara's teacher hadn't said much at the meeting so they weren't sure what to ask her. They really weren't certain what they should do next. It sounded to the parents like Ara would get more specialized help for a bit longer if he didn't get a diploma, but they always assumed that he would graduate from high school with a diploma.

QUESTIONS FOR REFLECTION

1. What could the school staff have done to assist Ara and his family in preparing for the developmental transition point of graduation? (CC2KI)
2. What are the implications for Ara if he does not graduate with a diploma? (CC1K2)
3. How could the staff have handled this situation differently so that the family could better process the information presented to them about transition planning, certificates of completion, and exit exams? (CC6K2)

Are They Ready?

BY GLENNA STEWART

Mr. Kim has seen the expectation for his pre-K students change dramatically over the years as the children were required to acquire more academic abilities in order to be ready for kindergarten. Mr. Kim was concerned that, although the students with disabilities were chronologically the right age for kindergarten, a few were not quite ready to transition to kindergarten.

Mr. Kim noted that according to state standards, readiness was linked directly to prereading skills, such as concepts about print. Although his students were progressing in this area of prereading, most students still struggled significantly. Also, Mr. Kim thought his students lacked the developmentally appropriate social-emotional or psychomotor skills that could be necessary for the transition to kindergarten. He felt that a child's development in each of these domains was as important for a successful transition as academic readiness.

Additionally, the teacher was worried that the teaching environment in kindergarten would require that the students sit and work independently for periods of time. Mr. Kim didn't think his students were ready for this. He noted that many of his students had difficulty following classroom rules, especially the one about keeping their hands to themselves, and that some of the children experienced delays in fine motor skills, such as cutting and coloring.

Although Mr. Kim was excited about the opportunity for many of his students to transition to a general education kindergarten class, he wasn't positive how to ensure their readiness. How can Mr. Kim determine if a child is ready?

*Q*UESTIONS FOR REFLECTION

1. What are some instructional suggestions for ensuring a child's readiness and for assisting him or her in successfully transitioning into kindergarten? (CC2K5)
2. How important is it for students to be "developmentally ready" for kindergarten? Is it equally important for students with and without disabilities? (CC2K5)

He's Not Autistic, Is He?

BY KIM MARTIN

In preschool, Daniel tended to throw tantrums when things did not go his way. He had difficulty with expressive language and trouble picking up academic concepts. He was evaluated through the local state agency charged with supporting preschool-aged students with disabilities and then the school district. Daniel was found to have some behaviors typical of children with autism, such as having tantrums when things did not go his way. "But lots of children have tantrums," thought the teacher. Since Daniel also exhibited additional behaviors that suggested autism, that diagnosis was given. Daniel showed progress during his early schooling experience, and by first grade, the team was impressed with his success in the classroom.

Daniel's first-grade general education teacher noted some behaviors that typified students with autism, like the need for clear schedules and difficulty with transitions. When things did not go as planned, Daniel was not ready to handle the "bumps" that came his way. Yet, his teacher noted the ease with which one could help him move through his tantrums. In the meantime, Daniel had passed the district reading assessment for all general education students in first grade. Additionally, he was proficient on the required timed math test, scoring 68 of 70 correct in under eight minutes. Daniel was evolving into an independent worker with limited behavior problems. His first-grade teacher inquired of the IEP team, "He's not autistic, is he?"

$\mathcal{Q}$UESTIONS FOR REFLECTION

1. Does the label of *autism* seem warranted in this situation? What are the benefits and limitations of Daniel having this label? (CC2K6)
2. Now that Daniel is performing at grade level and displaying limited behavior challenges, what transitional steps might the IEP team take? (CC2K5)

Is Medication the Right Thing?

Mr. Solis, a first-grade teacher, was amazed at the difference he saw in Hyun. Hyun had always had such trouble sitting still when the students were doing deskwork, and now, here Hyun was sitting and quietly working for what seemed like a really long time. Mr. Solis had wondered if it would really make a difference when Hyun's parents said they were going to start giving her medication, but now he could see the difference for himself.

He wondered about some of his other students. The three boys in the back row always seemed to get extra wiggly in the afternoon. He had tried moving them up to the front of the room but this hadn't seemed to help. Sitting near the back, they could get a little wiggly and it didn't seem to bother the other students, so Mr. Solis had moved them back again. Tana always had trouble paying attention right before lunch and sometimes here and there across the school day. Tamika also had trouble following classroom routines—so much so that Mr. Solis had talked to her mother about whether this occurred at home. Tamika's mom said that she hadn't seen such problems at home. Before and after school, Tamika helped care for the younger children in her family and the children next door, and Tamika's Mom said she did this very well.

Mr. Solis knew that more and more kids at the school were starting to be referred to their doctors to explore the need for medication to treat their attention problems, and this worried Mr. Solis. He thought medication was often just a quick fix for frustrated parents and teachers. He also wondered if there were things he did in the classroom that led to some of the problems he saw since, for example, Tamika didn't seem to have the problems at home that she had at school. Yet now, he was witnessing Hyun working diligently and producing better work than she had all year. Maybe it would help some of his other students. He wondered how best to decide when medication is the right thing for a student.

*Q*UESTIONS FOR REFLECTION

1. What factors should be considered before giving children medication to treat their disability? What role should a teacher play in this process? (CC2K7)
2. How can Mr. Solis figure out the difference between an age-appropriate problem with paying attention and a problem that might be helped with medication? (CC2K5)
3. How might differences between expectations at school and home, including cultural expectations, influence issues such as paying attention in class? How can a teacher respond to these issues? (CC2K3)

CHAPTER FOUR

....

Individual Learning Differences

*T*he vignettes in this chapter reflect CEC Standard 3 as they are related to the multiple interactions that occur between individual learning differences, cultural traditions, and primary language abilities of individuals with identified disabilities. These vignettes show how effective teachers use this knowledge of individual differences to guide decision making about meaningful and challenging learning opportunities for individuals with disabilities.

Selected CEC Common Core Standards: #3 Individual Learning Differences

CC3K1   Effects an exceptional condition(s) can have on an individual's life

CC3K2   Impact of learners' academic and social abilities, attitudes, interests, and values on instruction and career development

CC3K3   Variations in beliefs, traditions, and values across and within cultures and their effects on relationships among individuals with exceptional learning needs

CC3K4   Cultural perspectives influencing the relationships among families, schools, and communities as related to instruction

CC3K5   Differing ways of learning by individuals with exceptional learning needs, including those from culturally diverse backgrounds, and strategies for addressing these differences

She Can't Read?

Carrie's parents were so proud of her when she started reading. At age 2, she had been diagnosed as having a developmental delay, and since that time, they were never sure what to expect from her. They thought back to last year when, at the IEP meeting, her special education teacher had said that she wasn't going to put reading goals on Carrie's IEP because "kids like Carrie can't learn to read." This surprised Carrie's parents because Carrie had had reading goals in the previous year but the teacher said she had tried to teach Carrie and Carrie hadn't learned. Now, the teacher said, it was too late and from her experience, she repeated, "Kids like Carrie can't learn to read." Carrie's parents didn't like to take "no" for an answer and they also had high expectations for Carrie, so they decided to do something about this.

Carrie's older brother had been seeing a tutor, Mrs. Els, for enrichment activities and he had really liked working with the tutor. Carrie's parents liked her too and thought Mrs. Els had a gift for teaching. They didn't know if she knew anything about special education but decided to see if Mrs. Els would try to teach Carrie to read. Mrs. Els immediately said she would work with Carrie and she thought for sure that Carrie could learn to read.

Three times a week, Carrie's mom would pick up Carrie after school and drive her to Mrs. Els's tutoring center. Mrs. Els would work with Carrie for an hour and then Carrie's mother would drive her home. Carrie was always happy to go see Mrs. Els and always happy when she left. Sometimes Carrie's mom got a little tired of all the driving but Mrs. Els kept reporting that they were making progress, so Carrie's mom felt the driving was worth it overall.

When she started, Mrs. Els wasn't sure what reading approach was going to work best with Carrie, so she quickly moved away from the idea of spending hours teaching Carrie letter and sound combinations without the necessary context. She wanted to find an approach that would be motivating for Carrie, and actually get her wanting to read. Carrie had a few favorite words that she liked to use. Mrs. Els decided to teach Carrie the sounds associated with the letters in these words. Working from this approach, Mrs. Els was eventually able to teach Carrie the letters of the alphabet and their corresponding sounds. Carrie was motivated to read these few key words and liked to practice them regularly. At the end of the first year, when Carrie was actually reading, her mom knew that all the driving was well worth it!

ℚUESTIONS FOR REFLECTION

1. What beliefs and stereotypes about individuals with disabilities might limit opportunities such as that presented by the situation with Carrie's special education teacher? (CC3K3)
2. Discuss the impact this particular approach to instruction had for Carrie. What are some other approaches Mrs. Els could have used? (CC3K2)

Please Try before Referring

BY GLENNA STEWART

Mrs. Nguyen was a new resource teacher at an elementary school. One of her duties was to attend prereferral student study team meetings on a weekly basis. During these meetings, Mrs. Nguyen often heard the classroom teacher express frustration about specific learning problems and behaviors of the students in their classroom. It was always insightful to hear the recommendations of other staff members, and in many cases, the advice that was offered was substantial and practical.

Unfortunately, sometimes the recommendations made were met by resistance from the referring teacher. The referring teachers often felt that they had done everything they possibly could to help a student. Additional recommendations by staff were viewed with skepticism. The typical response to the suggestions was something like, "Been there, done that."

As far as the referring teacher was concerned, the recommendations, although well intentioned, were often viewed as just one more added thing to do in a day that was already totally consumed by teaching to the standards. If a student could not keep up, or took too much of the teacher's time, it was obvious to the teacher that the child must need special education services.

Mrs. Nguyen knew that her school was committed to appropriately identifying students with disabilities. At the same time, however, she worried about the referral of students to eligibility assessment for special education without the referring teacher providing evidence of response to the treatment interventions that were supposedly used. How could she help the teachers see that addressing individual needs was not just "one more thing" they had to do but rather an essential part of being a good teacher?

QUESTIONS FOR REFLECTION

1. How can Mrs. Nguyen work with the teachers to help them meet individual needs without them feeling overwhelmed? (CC3K2)
2. Given the diverse learning styles of individuals, what factors might a team consider when developing an appropriate intervening treatment? (CC3K5)

Don't Judge a Book by Its Cover

BY REBECCA DENNIS

It was the beginning of the school year, and Mr. Lance was busy getting to know his new routine and new students. He had a new group of students coming in to the middle school and he had enjoyed meeting them and their parents at their homes over the summer. He was ready to get started with the new school year.

As the first period bell rang, Mr. Lance noticed one of his new students and her parents in the hallway. Curious, he stepped outside to see if they needed help. The parents explained that they were looking for their daughter's room. When Mr. Lance told them that they had found the right room, the parents looked surprised. They stated that they had glanced in the classroom and so they thought there was a mistake. When Mr. Lance asked why they thought there had been a mistake, the parents replied, "Our child shouldn't be in the retarded room." Stunned, Mr. Lance asked why they thought that about his class. They replied, "Isn't it obvious? All of those children are in wheelchairs."

*Q*UESTION FOR REFLECTION

1. How can Mr. Lance respond to these parents' view about other types of disabilities? What information should Mr. Lance have shared with the family during their summer meeting to have avoided this exchange? (CC3K3)

Mrs. E. (that's what everyone called her) sat in her car and laughed. She had just completed a home visit that ended with the realization that she had been jumping to conclusions about the cultural beliefs of the family of Huong. Huong had been her student for a year now and she had been working with the family to clarify future goals and expectations for Huong as they began the process of planning his transition from school to postsecondary services. Over the course of her year's interactions with the family, Mrs. E. had noticed that Huong's family members tended to wait on him hand and foot. He didn't perform any household chores. This all concerned Mrs. E. because she thought it was important for him to develop more independence. This had led Mrs. E. to develop a long-term plan to inform Huong's family about the benefits of having Huong learn to take care of more of his own personal needs and contribute to household chores. She gently raised this issue whenever she could but tried not to be too pushy.

In preparation for their upcoming IEP meeting, Mrs. E. planned a home visit with Huong's family. She had been unable to arrange for an interpreter but Huong's college-age sister had answered the phone and volunteered to serve as interpreter. At the prearranged time, Mrs. E. arrived at the family home and began to ask about annual goals and objectives the family would like to see for Huong. She found the family to have lots of ideas for Huong in all areas except for the domestic area. She decided to be a little more forceful and asked about possible chores Huong could learn to do around the house or ways she could help him learn skills such as laundry or buying clothes. She asked several times but the family did not support any of the ideas she shared.

After the meeting was completed, Mrs. E. walked out to her car and Huong's sister asked to go with her. His sister asked Mrs. E. why those domestic skills seemed so important to her, and Mrs. E. shared with her what she had learned from the adult service agency staff about skills that were important for independent living. Huong's sister said she believed her family would want Huong to live independently but said they wouldn't want him to learn those domestic skills. In their family, only the women performed those tasks. All along, Mrs. E. had assumed that the family was being too protective of Huong due to his disability and hadn't considered different cultural views of gender roles. This is why she laughed when she got in the car. She knew that her cultural sensitivity wasn't quite as developed as she had thought!

*Q*UESTIONS FOR REFLECTION

1. Summarize the key cultural perspectives that Mrs. E seemed to have. How were these ultimately contrary to the family's desires? (CC3K4)
2. What could Mrs. E. have done to avoid jumping to the wrong conclusion about Huong's family's beliefs? (CC3K3)

I Hate My 504 Plan!

BY KIM MARTIN

Billy, now in middle school, was diagnosed in second grade as having attention deficit hyperactivity disorder (ADHD). He was referred for special education eligibility but the team found that with medication prescribed by his doctor, he was performing well in school. The team therefore determined that he did not qualify for services under IDEIA, but a 504 Plan was written to document needed interventions. When Billy graduated from elementary school he was reading at grade level.

In middle school, Billy began having problems with his grades. He did poorly on long-term assignments and missed items on rubrics, which resulted in low grades. Billy was not detail oriented, perceived long-term assignments as being overwhelming, and received little support from his teachers to make things easier. At the end of seventh grade, Billy was tested again and found to have a learning disability. Although he qualified for special education services under IDEIA at this point, Billy and his mother were adamant that he not be offered these services. Billy didn't want to be labeled as a "resource student." Instead, the school wrote a 504 accommodation plan for him.

The 504 Plan included ways to make Billy's learning environment easier for him. For example, he was allowed to dictate ideas into a tape recorder and the required length of writing assignments was lessened. Parents were to be notified of missing assignments or of grades lower than a C. This plan was revisited as Billy graduated from eighth grade and headed for high school.

In high school, the 504 Plan seemed to have little value. Although his teachers knew about it, the contents of the plan were not executed well. Billy's parents were not being contacted about missing assignments and low grades. In ninth grade, Billy was being pulled out of class for certain assessments, but these accommodations were not listed on his 504 Plan. Calls to the counselor by his mother were unanswered since Billy's counselor was on maternity leave.

About this time, Billy mentioned to his parents that he had had enough of the 504 Plan. He wanted it gone. His parents felt that since it was a safeguard of sorts, is should be left in place. As Billy's high school years went on, however, the 504 Plan continued to be ignored by his teachers and by Billy. Although the documented plan remained, it did not impact Billy's learning environment.

QUESTIONS FOR REFLECTION

1. What impact will Billy's attitude about support and services potentially have on his final school success and career development? (CC3K2)
2. What steps might Billy's mother take to ensure his success this final year in school? (CC3K3)
3. How do 504 Plans and IEPs differ in terms of how they address student learning differences? What are the implications of receiving services under Section 504 of the Vocational Rehabilitation Act or IDEIA? (CC3K1)

Placement Tug-of-War

BY KIM MARTIN

When Lola began first grade, her teacher was concerned about her communication patterns. Although Lola was able to complete much of the grade-level work, she did not communicate with her peers and only gave responses when called on, using one- or two-word responses. Toward the middle of the year, Lola's mother provided the school with some information from a local child development center. The diagnosis information from the center was that Lola had a speech and language impairment.

The school then conducted an assessment of Lola and found that she qualified for special education services. Although Lola was doing well in the first grade general education class, the IEP team thought that she would benefit from support provided by the resource teacher and the speech and language specialist. At first, Lola's mother agreed with the general education placement, then the next day, she decided that since Lola was essentially nonverbal, she wanted her in the protected environment of a self-contained special education class where either the teacher or the paraeducator was with Lola at all times. After much debate, the team went along with this decision and started this self-contained special education placement in second grade

Lola's second-grade special education teacher had a new challenge on her hands. Lola was doing so well in her self-contained class that, in fact, she was almost bored. Her teacher gave her extra work and she finished that work quickly. When the IEP team met, they again discussed the continuum of placement options for Lola. And again, Lola's mother was adamant about the more restrictive option because she thought Lola needed more intense support. Her teacher was afraid that Lola would be forever stuck in a special education classroom that she might not need. This seemed to be a placement tug-of-war.

QUESTIONS FOR REFLECTION

1. How can the school team make clear how supports can be brought to the general education class to meet Lola's unique learning needs? (CC3K2)
2. How can the school site better understand Lola's mother's concerns about a less restrictive placement? (CC3K4)

Who's to Blame?

BY KIM UFHOLTZ

Sean came into the world three months early, weighing only 1.5 pounds. During his first years he faced many developmental hurdles without many interventions for support. Sean's parents felt that he had overcome those early difficulties and would be fine in the future.

When Sean started kindergarten, he showed academic delays as he had difficulty grasping new concepts. He repeated that year because the school district thought this was an appropriate intervention, given Sean's lack of early childhood education. Sean relocated with his parents that next year and started first grade in a new school.

By second grade, his teacher, Ms. Smith, was very concerned about his fine motor development. Sean was not able to write his name or independently button his jacket. Additionally, Sean's speech delays were interfering with his social development. Ms. Smith was very concerned about the multiple needs Sean had that didn't seem to be sufficiently addressed. Why hadn't the district provided the needed services in these different areas? Why wasn't this family connected with outside agencies for support? Who was to blame for these missing services?

QUESTIONS FOR REFLECTION

1. Given the unique learning needs of Sean, what support should Ms. Smith help the family access? (CC3K1)
2. Describe strategies for addressing Sean's mobility and social abilities to increase classroom participation and his interaction with peers. (CC3K2)

What Do We Do Now?

BY KIM MARTIN

Jibril is a 9-year-old male with muscular dystrophy. Since kindergarten, Jibril has struggled with the basic academic tasks. Over the summer between second and third grade, Jibril's parents felt that his physical condition was deteriorating. Jibril could no longer get up from the carpet during group lessons, so a physician recommended that he be seated in a chair of unspecified height during these times. His parents felt that other physical accommodations needed to be made as well, although these were not specific recommendations from a physician or physical therapist. An IEP meeting was called to discuss the needed physical adaptations to Jibril's school environment. The school team suggested that Jibril be moved to a school that was prepared to meet the physical accommodations he required. That campus served a good number of children who were orthopedically impaired.

His parents wanted to keep Jibril with his current teacher and at his neighborhood school and see the physical accommodations made to for his specific needs. The school team wasn't sure the current placement could best meet Jibril's needs. They wondered, "What do we do now?"

QUESTION FOR REFLECTION

1. What possible solutions could the team come up with, given the different perspectives they have on Jibril's appropriate placement? Should Jibril have to leave his neighborhood school to receive his needed physical accommodations? Why or why not? (CC3K3)

Another Episode

BY JENNIFER KAGY

Once again, John had an "episode." This time, however, it did not occur in the classroom or on the playground, but rather in the school library. From what Mrs. Herkins, John's fourth-grade teacher could gather, John was upset because he could not find books on Victorian architecture. Thus, John became enraged and kicked over a small bookshelf and threatened to knock over more. Mrs. Herkins, quick on her feet, had to restrain John before more damage was done.

Meanwhile, the classroom aide escorted John's classmates quickly out of the library, following the guidelines of the "safety plan" that John's school support team developed in response to such "episodes." Once John calmed down, he picked up the mess that he had made and started to cry. He apologized profusely to Mrs. Herkins, as well as to the librarian and the principal who was now at the scene. In between his sobs, John was remorseful and repeatedly blamed his actions on his bipolar/schizophrenia disorder.

Although Mrs. Herkins felt bad for John, she did not know what else to do. It seemed that everything in her classroom had turned upside-down ever since John entered into her room six months ago. The current behavior plan (one of many) developed at John's last "emergency" IEP meeting was simply not working. Furthermore, Mrs. Herkins felt as if she had no support from the special education support teacher, her administrator, or the school psychologist. She had the feeling that she was expending all of her energy on John, and that the rest of her students were suffering as a result. As she reflected on the situation, she wondered if she had the energy left needed to effectively implement the current behavior plan. For the first time in her five-year career, Mrs. Herkins felt frustrated and somewhat bitter about having such a challenging student as John in her class. Although she tried to remain professional and implement "best practices," she found it very difficult without the support of the other IEP team members.

QUESTION FOR REFLECTION

1. How can the team members work together to better support John in his areas of need so that he can effectively access a variety of school and nonschool environments? (CC3K1)

CHAPTER FIVE

....

Instructional Strategies

*T*he vignettes in this chapter reflect CEC Standard 4 as they provide examples of some of the issues teachers face as they implement instruction to fit each of their students' individual strengths and needs. They demonstrate the challenges that teachers face as they attempt to implement evidence-based instructional strategies to adapt and modify the general education curriculum and any special education curriculum as well. The standard states that effective teachers use these strategies to enhance critical thinking and problem solving as well as the self-awareness, self-control, and self-esteem of their students.

Selected CEC Common Core Standards: #4 Instructional Strategies

CC4S1   Strategies to facilitate integration into various settings

CC4S3   Selection, adaptation, and use of instructional strategies and materials according to characteristics of the individual with exceptional learning needs

CC4S4   Strategies to facilitate maintenance and generalization of skills across learning environments

CC4S5   Procedures to increase the individual's self-awareness, self-management, self-control, self-reliance, and self-esteem

CC4S6   Strategies that promote successful transitions for individuals with exceptional learning needs.

Packaged Programs Are Not "Special"

BY ROBERT MARKEL

Mr. Hall has been a special educator at Jackson School for five years. Over the course of those five years, Mr. Hall has received training in several packaged language arts and math programs that have been acquired by the district. It seems like every year there is a new program that Mr. Hall must learn and teach to his students. In addition, the programs that he is required to use have not been designed for students with disabilities and are not always easily adapted. Yet, he is required to use the program and all its components.

Throughout Mr. Hall's special education training at the university he has been taught how to individualize interventions and adapt or modify materials to meet student needs. However, the program specialist at Jackson School, along with district representatives, has stated that the program is not to be modified. This goes against everything that Mr. Hall has learned in his credential preparation courses and student teaching. More importantly, Mr. Hall's students are struggling with the program and are showing little growth. Additionally, the activities required in the program are not representative of the IEP goals that have been developed. Mr. Hall is frustrated because he must share with parents that students have not met their goals because of insufficient opportunities to do so. The time and pacing requirements, directives from administration, and intensity of the program do not allow Mr. Hall time to individually assess and plan for interventions.

QUESTION FOR REFLECTION

1. Where can Mr. Hall gather information about additional curricula or specialized materials or adapting the resources he is currently required to use to better meet his student's needs? How could he go about sharing with administrators the need for these individualized materials and strategies? (CC4S3)

Josh's Wasting Time

Josh is waiting for the third-period bell to ring so he can head to his job. He likes working at the bike shop and thinks it's time to stop wasting his time in high school. People at school had a meeting where they asked him what he wanted to do in school and after he graduated, but after he told them, no one seemed to do anything different to help him. They called it a "transition meeting" but it just seemed like one more meeting where everyone talked about him but no one really listened to him. No one seems to care if he's there at the school and no one seems to care about what he wants to do. They don't seem to care if he learns and they don't teach anything he needs to know. Josh thinks that if he dropped out, he could work more hours and help the family more by bringing home a bigger pay-check. He knows his dad doesn't want him to drop out because he thinks he'll hang around with gangbangers. Josh just wants to work and spend his time doing something that makes sense to him. Maybe today is the day he leaves and never comes back. He thinks, "Maybe today," as the bell rings.

QUESTIONS FOR REFLECTION

1. How should Josh's school team address Josh's concerns about school and his transition planning? (CC4S6)
2. How can Josh's school provide instruction to help him feel that school is not just a waste of his time? Should the school do this? (CC4S3)

Who Is Right?

....

BY JOLIE FOSTER-BERMAN

A kindergarten–first grade program for students with autism was set up in a district to support a group of students the district labeled as being "high functioning." When the school district developed this program, it was decided that after spending a year or two at this school with intensive supports for successful inclusion, the students would be expected to return to their home school. Because this means some students are expected to leave the school every year, most of the parents go to due process over the issue of this change in placement. The principal now feels resentful toward the program because of the time and aggravation involved in these due process proceedings. The principal has informed the district's special education administrators that she would like to discontinue the program at the school. She believes that the issue of money and time has become overwhelming. The principal has also stated that she is "protecting her teachers." She does not want the campus to have a high population of students with autism because the teachers would become frustrated.

The parents of the students with autism feel that their children have grown familiar with the setting and built friendships, so why should they leave? The special education teacher wonders if the program is setting the students up for failure by sending them back to their home school, because her students generally have problems with change. She isn't sure how to address the principal's concerns, the students' needs, the parents' wishes, and the district's plan. As a new teacher, she knows she can't rock the boat too much and therefore feels increasingly frustrated.

QUESTIONS FOR REFLECTION
....

1. Does this program seem to use strategies to facilitate integration into various settings? What, if anything, should be done differently? (CC4S1)
2. What kinds of strategies could be used to facilitate transitions within and between schools for the students in this program? (CC4S6)

Gilbert "Sounds" It Out

Ms. Valentine worries about Gilbert. The rest of the third-graders have picked up on the new phonics instruction that has been mandated by the state in which she teaches, and she wonders why Gilbert just doesn't seem to be able to make the letter-sound connection. She worries about this as she prepares each lesson and wonders if Gilbert will continue to fall behind. Ms. Valentine continues to worry about Gilbert as she teaches and starts to wonder about whether or not she should refer Gilbert for some extra help, as she's tried everything she can think of to help him understand the connections between letters and sounds.

Ms. Valentine is worrying about Gilbert today as she begins talking with the students about how to spell the word *tale,* reminding them that vowels need helpers to say their names. She asks the students to share the ways they think *tale* is spelled and then writes on the board the different ways they have decided it is spelled. One student says *T-A-L-L* and another says *T-I-L-E.* Still another says *T-E-L-L* and one adds *T-A-L-E.* Ms. Valentine asks if there are any other ideas about how to spell the word, but the children say no. She tries to take a moment to check on Gilbert, but she is also trying to attend to all of her students as they try to sound out the words and pick the correct spelling. When she asks them which spelling they think is correct, the students readily eliminate *T-A-L-L* and *T-I-L-E* as incorrect spellings because they don't have a helper friend and are the wrong vowel, but they aren't sure what to do about *T-E-L-L.* She asks the children to say the two words and listen for a difference. She asks, "Don't you hear the difference?" At that point Gilbert raises his hand and says, "They almost sound the same but they look different when someone says them." Ms. Valentine replies, "You're absolutely right, Gilbert" and tells all of the children to look for the difference and try to feel the difference. She now knows Gilbert feels the difference and she can use this skill to help him make the letter-sound connection.

*Q*UESTION FOR REFLECTION

1. What skills in self-assessment and problem solving has Gilbert demonstrated here? (CC4S2) How can these skills be generalized to other types of activities? (CC4S4)

Forgetting to Count

Ira was busy counting the raised dots on the page and writing the corresponding number on the line. The quiet music that Mr. Westfall, his special education resource teacher, played in the background of his resource room seemed to drown out the typical noises of a busy school. Ira sat next to the window and enjoyed taking a moment to look outside after completing each problem. Ira wasn't alone in the room, as Jamal and Paula were busy working on writing assignments at a different table. Mr. Westfall was moving back and forth between these two groups of students, ensuring that everyone was on task. Ira continued to work on his page of six problems. When he was finished, Mr. Westfall checked Ira's work and placed a star next to each problem that he got correct.

Ira then picked up the striped pencil he was using (everyone had a favorite pencil in Mr. Westfall's room) and moved onto his next task: solving addition problems. He was busy trying to do the problems without using the number line with the raised dots. After a number of failed attempts, Mr. Westfall reminded him how to use the number line they had developed just for him based on his individual needs and got him working again. Using the number line, Ira began counting out the problems correctly.

After working one-on-one with Mr. Westfall, it was time for Ira to transition back to his own general education classroom. His classmates were working independently on their own math assignments when Ira arrived. As previously arranged by Mr. Westfall, Ira went to his own desk to continue working on the addition problems he had previously started. His classroom teacher, Ms. Heideman, came by his desk to give him the number line with the raised dots that they kept in her class for Ira to use. Ms. Heideman spent a few minutes with Ira, trying to help him get adjusted back to class and on task.

At the end of the independent math period, Ms. Heideman collected everyone's math assignments. She took a moment to glace over the work Ira completed. Most of the problems were wrong. Taking a deep breath, Ms. Heideman asked herself how that could be. She had seen the work Ira completed with Mr. Westfall and was confused by the inconsistencies she saw in his work produced in her classroom. It seemed that every time Ira returned to her room, he forgot how to count!

$\mathcal{Q}$UESTIONS FOR REFLECTION

1. Identify some of the reasons Ira might be able to complete a task in one environment but not another. How could services be delivered in a different manner to help Ira transition? (CC4S6)
2. What are some strategies to facilitate generalization of skills across learning environments? (CC4S4)
3. What are some ways Ms. Heideman and Mr. Westfall can help Ira increase his independence with tasks when in her classroom? (CC4S5)

Teaching to Read

BY JOY DYE

Mr. Page began his first year of teaching at a high school. He was the special education support teacher for science, math, and history. He was very excited about starting his first teaching job. Mr. Page spent hours upon hours on his lesson plans, making sure that all the needs of the students were being met through his teaching. His students responded well to his style of teaching and he enjoyed providing pull-in supports in the general education classes. He was able to keep the students interested and engaged (most of the time).

After about a month of teaching, Mr. Page began to wonder if one of his students wasn't a functional reader. James always refused to read aloud and hardly ever turned in written assignments. Some other students were not able to read at grade level and their writing assignments had gross spelling errors, but they had basic reading and writing skills. Concerned about his possibly-not-reading student, Mr. Page began looking through James's records and reviewed his reading scores from previous tests that were administered. Mr. Page realized that he was correct. The records showed that James was reading at about the first-grade level, and his writing wasn't much better. Mr. Page wondered how this had not been addressed in previous IEPs and was determined to monitor the situation.

By the time the school year was underway, Mr. Page had formed a good relationship with James. One day, James came in to see Mr. Page at the end of the school day. Nervously, James explained to him that he couldn't read and wanted to learn how to read but was too embarrassed to go through this process in front of all the other students. Mr. Page let James know that he would be honored to help him through this and that he would do everything he could to help him learn to read.

After James left his classroom, Mr. Page thought, "How in the world am I going to be able to do this? First of all, I have hardly any experience in teaching basic reading skills, since this isn't usually needed for my other high school-aged students. Second, I don't even have material to begin this process." One thing Mr. Page did know was that he did have the time available to do this. He could switch James into his third period, which was his planning period. This way, Mr. Page would be able to teach James without the worry of others knowing about his secret.

Mr. Page began to prepare for the task of gathering materials needed to teach reading and to research how to teach reading. He was a bit nervous, but also excited about the opportunity to help James.

QUESTIONS FOR REFLECTION

1. What sources could Mr. Page use to locate specialized materials, curricula, or resources to use with James? What type if reading methods might be appropriate for Mr. Page to use? (CC4S3)

2. How could a student have proceeded through school without having developed basic reading skills? (CC4S4)

How Far Can She Stretch?

BY JOY DYE

Mrs. Stone is a special education support teacher for 18 fourth-, fifth-, and sixth-grade students with mild to moderate learning disabilities. At the end of the first week of school, she was informed by her supervisor that on Monday she would also be supporting a nonverbal student who was described as being very low functioning and autistic. He was a fifth-grader and would be arriving with his personal one-on-one aide. Evidently, Alex's parents did not like the class he was currently in and they felt like the other students were hindering Alex's learning. They wanted him to be challenged.

Mrs. Stone was surprised by this turn of events because there was no transition period described, no prior introductions, nor exchange of information (except what she was told by her supervisor). On Monday, Alex came to school with his mother, his personal one-on-one aide, and Mrs. Stone's supervisor. The day began with a simple introduction, a brief review of Alex's prior learning experience, and then good-byes (except for Alex and his aide, who stayed).

After observing Alex during his first few hours in his fifth-grade class, Mrs. Stone knew she had a lot of work cut out for her. Alex was very different from her other students. He didn't speak; he uttered sounds that were unintelligible. He wasn't toilet trained and needed his aide to help him take care of himself. He constantly shook his hands in his face or in the faces of the other students. He didn't seem to understand personal space issues and frequently invaded other people's space. He could write his name and respond to his name, he tried to repeat simple phrases such as, "Hello," and he had a great smile. His smile was so beautiful that it was impossible not to smile in return. The smile really drew Mrs. Stone to Alex, but she wondered what to do, because she wasn't really trained to deal with the learning issues that Alex seemed to present.

One positive thing about this situation was that Alex's aide was very hardworking and had a natural talent for working with Alex. Now Mrs. Stone had a challenge before her. She read that Alex was able to identify all letters and numbers and could read at about the first-grade level (simple words and some sight words). She sat down with him and had him read to her; she could hear him read but it was very hard to understand. Alex always smiled and somewhat giggled throughout the reading. He had a very short attention span and wanted to touch and smell everything.

Mrs. Stone had to decide what she was going to do with Alex. Which reading group should Alex join? How would the other students respond to his behaviors? Should Alex just work individually with his one-on-one aide? There was so much to do and so many decisions to make. How was she going to meet Alex's needs without taking away from the other students? Alex just seemed so different from her other students and needed a lot of help. How far could she be stretched?

1. What are some of the instructional strategies that might work best for Mrs. Stone in supporting this diverse group of students? What would be some of the limitations she would experience with these different strategies? (CC4S3)
2. How can Mrs. Stone help Alex generalize his reading skill across learning environments? (CC4S4)

Finding the Right "Fit"

"Now, why isn't he in one of those really special classes?" After having just explained again what *full inclusion* was, Miss Johnson was exasperated to hear the second-grade teacher, Mr. Han, ask that question. Here it was, late October, and Samuel was still not a true member of this second-grade classroom. Samuel has autism. This label, this setting, and the things that made him uniquely Samuel were making this placement all the more challenging. Was it time for the IEP team to consider different supports or a different placement?

When approached last year by the principal about having Samuel in his classroom, Mr. Han was hesitant but accepting. In the past he had worked closely with Miss Johnson, the resource specialist, and thought he had a pretty good idea of how to work with a student who has special needs. What he wasn't prepared for was the level of involvement Samuel would require.

Samuel had been identified for special education services in first grade. He had arrived at the school site late in his kindergarten year and had begun the Student Study Team (SST) process at that point. Interventions for social, academic, and language support were provided. But during his first-grade year it was determined that Samuel would benefit from a complete evaluation. His parents were very hesitant from the beginning. They were leery of interventions and didn't initially want him qualified for special education but they were happy to see him receive collaborative services from the resource specialist.

By the end of first grade, the IEP team decided that Samuel would benefit from receiving more support, including 3.5 hours of aide support, weekly district support to both teachers and aide, as well as daily collaboration from the resource specialist. Now, here he was in second grade, and the level of support he was receiving didn't seem to be matching his needs. Samuel wasn't making the anticipated academic gains, his behavioral outbursts and agitation were increasing, and the lack of social acceptance by his peers was a cause for concern. Mr. Han was just honestly too overwhelmed with all the demands, interruptions, and planning. As Samuel's outbursts increased, so did Mr. Han's reluctance.

*Q*UESTIONS FOR REFLECTION

1. At this time, how could Miss Johnson address Mr. Han's concerns? What immediate actions might be needed to meet both the student's and the teacher's needs? (CC4S3)
2. What process could be used to examine the strategies that have been used and to identify those that have been effective and those that have not? (CC4S3)

Mr. Simms couldn't believe that he now was starting to think that his packaged reading program actually worked. He had complained to everyone he could think of when he was first required to use it, but they all told him that he was required to use the program because it was "research based." He couldn't see how he could address all his students' needs using this program. What about math goals? Social goals? Functional goals? How could this one program meet all the individual reading goals that his students had? Mr. Simms was told to "do the best he could," which he did, but he constantly worried that he was letting his students and their parents down.

The packaged reading program required Mr. Simms to engage in regular progress monitoring, which seemed like a lot of work at first. Gradually, he started to enjoy the time spent monitoring the students' progress because he saw just that—progress! By the end of the year, he saw that his students had made more progress than he had seen in all of his years of teaching. He was shocked because he had believed so strongly that it just wouldn't work. Mr. Simms couldn't wait to share the news with his students' parents, but he still wondered, What about math goals, social goals, functional goals? He knew he had tried to work on some of those goals but he had not been able to do an adequate job. Even though he was a "seasoned teacher," he felt he had to follow "orders" to teach the packaged reading program and that program only. Mr. Simms therefore felt he was faced with a real dilemma—keep using the program as directed and see real progress in one area but face the risk of not seeing progress in other areas of need.

QUESTIONS FOR REFLECTION

1. What are the benefits of such systematic approaches to teaching reading? How might it conflict with individual needs and learning styles? (CC4S3)
2. How could Mr. Simms incorporate student self-assessment into his progress monitoring activities? (CC4S2)
3. How can such packaged programs facilitate and interfere with generalization and maintenance of skills? (CC4S4)

What Was She Thinking?

Mrs. Hanks remembered back to last spring when she was told she would finally have an inclusion specialist to help her include students with disabilities in her fifth-grade class. She had been a fifth-grade teacher for years and had a special education credential but had always felt like she just needed a little more help to effectively include students with disabilities in her class. After her first meeting with the inclusion specialist, she had to just shake her head. The inclusion specialist seemed very nice and all, but she had simply dropped off a box of supplies that she told Mrs. Hanks she could use for the students included in her class. The inclusion specialist proudly talked about how hard she had worked all summer to create these boxes for each grade level in the district. She had delivered almost all the boxes and so felt she was ready to face the new challenges that would come with the new school year. She told Mrs. Hanks that she hoped she liked the box and then left, saying she would contact Mrs. Hanks again sometime soon. Mrs. Hanks didn't know what to say.

She didn't want to sound ungrateful, but as Mrs. Hanks looked through the materials in the box, she couldn't imagine how she would use most of it. Most of the materials didn't match the curriculum materials she currently used in her class. The content standards were reflected but not the actual materials she used, nor did they fit with her active teaching style. They also didn't match the needs of the students with disabilities who were to be included in her class for the coming year. She wondered if this reflected the inclusion specialist's overall view of how she would be supporting Mrs. Hanks for the coming year. This really was not the kind of support that Mrs. Hanks felt would help her with effectively including students.

QUESTIONS FOR REFLECTION

1. How could the inclusion specialist have attended to appropriate individualized adaptations for Mrs. Hanks's students? (CC4S3)
2. What effect might such generalized, mismatched adaptations have on the self-esteem of children with disabilities included in Mrs. Hanks's classroom? Might the students feel out of place? (CC4S5)

CHAPTER SIX
....

Learning Environments and Social Interactions

The vignettes in this chapter reflect CEC Standard 5 as they provide examples of some of the issues teachers face as they manage the teaching and learning environment. The vignettes demonstrate how effective teachers create a safe, positive, supportive, and age-appropriate learning environment by effectively using space, time, materials, equipment, and technology. They demonstrate how effective teachers assist students to interact with the culturally diverse population found in the world today. The vignettes also demonstrate how specialist educators help their general education colleagues to effectively integrate students with disabilities to create a sense of community. Examples of crisis intervention and coordination of the efforts of paraeducators and volunteers and tutors are also provided.

Selected CEC Common Core Standards: #5 Learning Environments and Social Interactions

CC5K3   Effective management of teaching and learning
CC5K4   Teacher attitudes and behaviors that influence behavior of individuals with exceptional learning needs
CC5S12   Design and management of daily routines
CC5S14   Mediation of controversial intercultural issues among students within the learning environment in ways that enhance any culture, group, or person
CC5S15   Structure, direct, and support the activities of paraeducators, volunteers, and tutors

Did Katie Receive a Fair Chance?

BY JOY DYE

Mrs. Kell just received notice that she will be getting a new student. The psychologist and the special education resource teacher had just finished testing Katie, a kindergarten student, and determined that she was emotionally disturbed and would be placed directly into a self-contained special education class. The psychologist was the first to approach Mrs. Kell to let her know that he was going to recommend that Katie be placed in her class. Mrs. Kell's program specialist later invited her to Katie's IEP meeting, which was to be held next week.

During this week Mrs. Kell inquired about Katie. She wanted to know what abilities Katie had and what she would need to do to prepare her class for Katie in case everyone at the IEP meeting did decide to have Katie placed in her class. After speaking to the psychologist, Mrs. Kell was amazed to find that Katie had attended kindergarten for only two weeks and was then given home teaching. At the principal's request, Katie had been placed on home teaching until testing was completed. Evidently, Katie had hit two boys in the face and wasn't able to "settle in" to the classroom environment. There were few formal records available to help figure out why this incident had occurred, but the psychologist said the parents had reported that they had had a lot of trouble with Katie at home.

Mrs. Kell thought this was an odd situation. She wasn't sure that Katie was really given a fair chance to make it in the general education setting. Instead of making modifications, providing additional support, and possibly moving Katie to a class with a more experienced teacher, the team decided it was best for Katie to stay home until testing was completed.

QUESTIONS FOR REFLECTION

1. Instead of being placed on home teaching right away, what suggestions would you give to help make Katie's first year of formal school a success? (CC5K4, CC5S4)
2. Mrs. Kell isn't sure the psychologist's recommendation is the best for Katie. What data might need to be collected to help suggest needed modifications to her learning environment? (CC5S6)

What's an Aide to Do?

Felicia threw her book across the room and hit Tyrell in the back of the head again.

Mr. Sanders looked up from the small reading group he was instructing and frowned. How had this happened again? Ms. Wang, Felicia's one-on-one aide, was sitting right there. Why had Felicia thrown the book again? Mr. Sanders had gone to great lengths to explain to Ms. Wang that such behavior could not be allowed in the classroom. He expressed that it was Ms. Wang's job to ensure that Felicia did not endanger herself or any of the other 19 second-graders in the room. It seemed like an easy enough job.

Ms. Wang spent her next 10-minute break pacing back and forth in frustration. She didn't understand why Felicia had thrown the book. She knew that Felicia had the diagnosis of "learning disabilities" and that people always said that she must also have a behavior disorder even if that had never been written down on formal forms. Ms. Wang also had been given a "behavior plan" that she was supposed to follow but it didn't really help her figure out how to help Felicia. One minute she was trying to get Felicia to point to the picture of the word she had just said, and the next thing she knew, the book was flying. Ms. Wang knew that Felicia was bored with this task, but she didn't know what else to do with her. She was supposed to do some kind of a reading activity for 30 minutes while Mr. Sanders taught the rest of the class, but Ms. Wang was out of ideas. She recalled her brief meetings with the special education resource program teacher, where she was continually reminded to "modify" work so that it looked like second-grade work. But how was she supposed to do that? Mr. Sanders wasn't able to help answer this question, as he had never worked with a student who required that much support. He was awfully nice to Ms. Wang and seemed to handle Felicia's outbursts without getting upset at Felicia or Ms. Wang. But nobody had told Ms. Wang how to predict Felicia's physical outbursts, or what to do to prevent them. She just wasn't sure what to do!

QUESTIONS FOR REFLECTION

1. What training and support should be provided for Ms. Wang, the aide, so she could assist Felicia in developing appropriate behaviors and learn from the curriculum? What difficulties do you see with the use of one-on-one aide support such as that provided for Felicia? (CC5S15)
2. What steps should be taken to prevent and intervene in a crisis situation when Felicia has an outburst? (CC5K6)
3. What aspects of effective inclusive models are absent in this case study? (CC5S3)
4. What other models of support should be considered for Felicia? (CC5S2)

How Does Ned Fit In?

BY KELLY CARTER-SKILLMAN

Ned is in kindergarten for the second year. He has been diagnosed with multiple disabilities and experiences a set of varied learning challenges. He also has a great smile! Ned had difficulties in school during his first year in kindergarten and so his parents wanted him to repeat kindergarten. His IEP team decided that he needed more support to be successful in kindergarten and so he was assigned a full-time one-on-one aide. Even though he has this full-time aide, Ned has been having difficulty in his kindergarten class. He spends a good bit of time rocking back and forth and swinging his arms from side to side, which distracts his classmates. He also frequently vocalizes in a low droning tone, which is also disruptive even though he sits way in the back of the classroom. As far as Mrs. Kendall, the kindergarten teacher, is concerned, Ned resists her help when she approaches him and he also resists help from his classmates. The aide doesn't seem to have helped the situation much either. Ned seems to do fine when he leaves the classroom for occupational therapy and speech therapy, but Mrs. Kendall believes that he is just "shut down" in his kindergarten class. Because of this, Mrs. Kendall has referred Ned for placement in the self-contained special education class on campus.

Mrs. Kimura, the teacher of the self-contained special education class, was informed about this referral for a possible change in placement by the principal. The principal asked Mrs. Kimura to observe Ned in class and to review his IEP records and assessments to see what she thought about a change in placement. After observing him in his kindergarten class, Mrs. Kimura believed that Ned could be successful in his inclusive placement. She thought the services provided thus far just weren't a good match for Ned and his abilities and needs. When Mrs. Kimura reported this at a meeting with the principal and Mrs. Kendall, Mrs. Kendall said she disagreed and was adamant that Ned should be moved to the self-contained special education classroom. Mrs. Kimura said that she had some ideas about how to modify instruction for Ned and also thought they needed to develop a positive behavioral support plan for some of the troubling behaviors they had observed—but Mrs. Kendall said she didn't think it would do any good.

*Q*UESTIONS FOR REFLECTION

1. What additional supports might Ned need to help him be successful in his inclusive placement? What process should be used to determine the supports? (CC5S3)
2. What are some support strategies and teaching strategies that might be presented to Mrs. Kendall? (CC5K2)
3. What impact might Mrs. Kendall's negative attitude be having on Ned's perceived success? (CC5K4)

How Far Can an Aide Go?

BY KIM MARTIN

Mrs. Rajoub is a one-on-one aide for Kim, an 8-year-old girl who has been given the label of autism. Mrs. Rajoub was hired by the district based on a request from Kim's family. Kim's special education support teacher, Mrs. Hancock, was informed that an aide would be provided for Kim on the first day that Mrs. Rajoub showed up to work with Kim. Mrs. Hancock feels like she has been "two steps behind" since Mrs. Rajoub arrived because she has had difficulty finding time to train Mrs. Rajoub.

A particular problem has arisen in regard to Kim's positive behavioral support plan. Although affectionate with Kim, Mrs. Rajoub has difficulty implementing the structured plan. Mrs. Hancock has to repeatedly intervene as Mrs. Rajoub works with Kim because Mrs. Rajoub's affectionate interventions tend to make Kim lose focus on her learning activities. Since Mrs. Rajoub was hired with input from Kim's family and is the support person who spends the most time with Kim, Mrs. Rajoub believes it is important to communicate regularly with the family. However, she often gives the family erroneous information and complains about Mrs. Hancock's frequent interruptions. Mrs. Hancock is frustrated because she is trying to develop a relationship with the family herself and is also trying to be sure that the behavioral support plan that the team, including Kim's family, helped to develop is followed. She's held multiple training sessions with the aide in regard to how to best implement the positive behavioral support plan and has held several team meetings, but none of the ideas they've tried seem to alleviate the problems.

QUESTIONS FOR REFLECTION

1. What could Mrs. Hancock have done differently in training Mrs. Rajoub? What additional supports might she still need to offer Mrs. Rajoub? (CC5S15)
2. What cultural factors might influence Mrs. Rajoub's interactions with Kim? How can Mrs. Hancock respect those cultural factors? In general, how can cultural mismatches between school and home impact the development of behavioral intervention plans? (CC5K8)

Study Skills or Homework?

BY JOY DYE

Mrs. Graves has taught in a seventh- and eighth-grade special education resource program for the past two years. She provided support in English and math classes. She also had one period a day for a class she called "Study Skills." Each year she was never happy with her study skills period. She wanted this time to be used to help her students learn basic study skills that would help them in all their classes. Instead, this class ended up being a homework or project catch-up class. It seemed to take a life of its own and was out of her control; there was no time for study skills to be taught. Mrs. Graves knew it was time for a change but didn't quite know what to change.

Mrs. Graves knew that her students needed to be taught study skills such as organizing notes and assignments, studying for tests and quizzes, and learning strategies to find the big idea of each chapter. But she also saw the need to provide support with the variety of assignments on which the students were working. This presented a great problem because there were up to 28 students who shared up to six teachers, which meant many different assignments, homework, projects, due dates, and grading rubrics. She also found that she could not rely on the students to be completely aware of the different assignments. So that meant that she needed to figure out a better system for gathering assignments from the six different teachers so that she could stay ahead of the game. Mrs. Graves seemed to be over-whelmed with a lot of information; however, she knew that with all the knowledge she had, there had to be a solution out there.

QUESTIONS FOR REFLECTION

1. Should Mrs. Graves focus on teaching study skills or helping students complete their homework assignments? How can she manage incorporating all of these teaching and learning goals in her study skills class? (CC5K3)
2. What should be expected of the students in terms of gathering information about and completing projects? How can Mrs. Graves foster self-advocacy and independence in this area? (CC5S2, CC5S9)
3. How can Mrs. Graves better establish a consistent classroom routine to assist the students in completing their assignments for their core courses? How can she best gather information from all of the teachers who work with her students? (CC5S12)

Going around in Circles

BY KIM UFHOLTZ

Tom is diagnosed as having attention deficit hyperactivity disorder. He completed his first attempt at kindergarten with support from the special education resource teacher. Because he didn't make as much progress as expected, the IEP team next decided to develop a formal behavior intervention plan with the district-level behavior specialist, but the plan seemed to have little impact on Tom's classroom behavior. He continued to struggle academically, making no progress. All the attempts the district behavior specialist made to control his impulsive behavior were unsuccessful. The specialist then suggested isolating Tom from his peers during the majority of class instruction. This had some success in minimizing his impulsive outbursts but Ms. Brown's anxiety was increasing, as she was not sure how to best meet Tom's needs and those of her other students. She didn't think it was in Tom's best interests to receive all his instruction one-to-one, but without additional suggestions from the specialists she was at a loss of what to do.

Recess posed another set of problems for Tom, and the team decided to have him take his recess at an alternative time, away from all his peers. Ms. Brown knew Tom was dismayed at not being allowed to play with his friends. Her concerns about his current placement and his behavior plan continued to grow.

Ms. Brown consulted once again with the school psychologist, who, again, reported to the IEP team that he felt the school was doing everything it could to support Tom's behavioral needs. She thought additional supports or recommendations would need to come from a medical evaluation. Tom's parents agreed to this.

Months passed as the school nurse tried to help the parents go through the process of making the appointment and applying for the needed insurance support. Glitches seemed to arise at every pass. As the school year was progressing and no change was taking place for Tom, Ms. Brown began to question if a more restrictive placement would be appropriate. Could he get more intense support in a more restrictive setting?

QUESTIONS FOR REFLECTION

1. Were the behavior interventions suggested appropriate for Tom? Were sufficient adaptations made to Tom's learning environment before the recommendation to change placement was made? (CC5S5)
2. How does a team determine the least intensive strategy to use in a situation like this? What are your thoughts on the role of medication in terms of least intrusive strategies? (CC5S11)

Michael Deserves a Chance

BY KELLY CARTER-SKILLMAN

Mrs. Skelton has been called to go help another special education teacher with a student who is displaying some very challenging behaviors. The student was a former one of hers and Mrs. Skelton knew that this student, Michael, age 10, could present challenges but was also responsive to appropriate interventions. He had a history of displaying aggressive behavior and a variety of diagnostic labels that didn't really help explain his aggressiveness. The principal thought that it would be a good idea for Mrs. Skelton to possibly assist Michael due to the good rapport she had with him and his family, since he appears to be having a lot of trouble adjusting to his new environment. Even though school has only started, his mother has already been called to pick him up six times.

As she approaches the classroom, Mrs. Skelton is greeted by a shoe flying past her. She sees the principal and special education teacher towering with arms crossed over a small figure crouched on the floor. Michael is sobbing. Mrs. Skelton observes desks turned over, books scattered, and a menagerie of school supplies all over the floor. "I already threatened to called the police on him," the principal booms. "He just doesn't seem to care. Mom is on her way to pick him up, once again. Next time it will be the police for sure." Michael's new teacher nods his head in agreement. It appears that Michael became aggressive when he asked to carry the emergency backpack out to the playground at the upcoming scheduled disaster drill. Michael was informed that it wasn't his turn, yet no other supports were offered to help him understand and accept this reason.

Mrs. Skelton is aware that the special education teacher is new to teaching students with moderate/severe disabilities and that the principal is new to supporting teachers in this field. However, Mrs. Skelton is quite frustrated with the fact that the only solution proposed is to constantly send the child home or to threaten calling the police! Additionally, the district behavior specialist has provided ongoing support to the new teacher. Yet, the teacher doesn't appear to be implementing any of the given strategies. Mrs. Skelton even heard him say, "I like the way I teach. It worked in my other classroom, and it can work here."

As Mrs. Skelton looks at the limp body on the floor, shoes off and exhausted, she takes a deep breath. At this point support has been offered by herself and a very qualified professional. To no avail, it appears to have been ignored. What is frightening to her is that the police have now been mentioned by the principal. What can Mrs. Skelton do to maintain professional rapport with the principal and this teacher while upholding the rights of the student?

*Q*UESTIONS FOR REFLECTION

59

CHAPTER 6

*Learning
Environments
and Social
Interactions*

1. Describe the impact the teacher's and principal's attitudes and actions might be having on Michael's behavior. (CC5K4)
2. How can this teacher develop a rapport with Michael? What impact might that have on his behavior? (CC5S7)
3. What strategies for appropriate crisis prevention and intervention should be in place in this classroom? (CC5K6, CC5S5)

Stop Teasing Me

BY KIM MARTIN

Ricky is a 10-year-old student diagnosed with a behavior disorder. He frequently displays hostile, aggressive behavior, especially when in less supervised arenas, like recess. Currently Ricky is under medical treatment for some of these behaviors.

Ricky is of Cambodian descent. His mother is Cambodian and speaks only Khmer. Ricky is protective of his mother and considers her the most important person in his life. His mother likes to visit the classroom frequently and watch Ricky when playing outside. His peers tease him about the way his mother talks and her presence at school. They enjoy saying insulting things about his mother, as they know that it is an especially sensitive area for Ricky.

Many times Ricky comes in after recess very upset and angry because of the things the other kids say about his mother. The teacher attempts to reassure Ricky by saying that it should not bother him because the children aren't really trying to insult his mother; they are just trying to tease him.

The problem has carried over into the classroom as well. Ricky cannot seem to settle down after recess. He becomes disruptive, belligerent, and hostile toward others in the class. He does not focus this behavior toward those who tease him; rather, everyone is a target. Ricky's teacher has tried to resolve this problem by sending him to another classroom for a cooling-off period. Often, even after this intervention and a chat with the teacher, Ricky cannot shake off his feelings of anger and resentment toward the other students at school.

*Q*UESTIONS FOR REFLECTION

1. What strategies could this teacher use to teach Ricky to give and receive meaningful feedback from his peers? (CC5S14)
2. Discuss schoolwide approaches to limit teasing of students with and without disabilities. (CC5S1)
3. How might this teacher help the students develop a respect for cultural differences? What changes to the learning environment might help facilitate this? (CC5S13)

CHAPTER SEVEN

....

Language

The vignettes in this chapter reflect CEC Standard 6 as they provide examples of issues teachers face as they address the language needs and abilities of their students. The expectation for teachers is that they understand the ways in which language development influences learning and instruction. Effective teachers use augmentative and alternative communication supports and match their instruction to the language abilities of their students. They also provide effective language models and assist learners whose primary language is not English.

Selected Common Core Standards: # 6 Language

CC6K1   Effects of cultural and linguistic differences on growth and development

CC6K2   Characteristics of one's own culture and use of language and the ways in which these can differ from other cultures and uses of languages

CC6K4   Augmentative and assistive communication strategies

CC6S1   Strategies to support and enhance communication skills of individuals with exceptional learning needs

CC6S2   Communication strategies and resources to facilitate understanding of subject matter for students whose primary language is not the dominant language

Can I Do It?

BY GLENNA STEWART

Mr. T. (as his students called him) was excited about trying the components of sheltered instruction in his classroom. He had just learned about sheltered instruction in his teacher preparation program and had read about how this instructional model can help learners who are learning English as a second language. He was certainly excited to try it with his students, as many of them were English language learners.

Although his lessons were carefully planned, Mr. T. found that many of his students had difficulty accessing the content he was presenting. He learned that sheltered instruction was designed to make language more comprehensible. It focused on student-centered learning rather than teacher-directed learning. Mr. T. knew these were components that needed to be added to his lesson preparation and delivery.

As Mr. T. reviewed the components of sheltered instruction, he discovered that components of this type of instruction focused on building a foundation for student learning. Academic language is explicitly taught in each curricular area. Students are provided with concrete examples of new concepts, carefully linked to their prior knowledge. Specific tools and strategies were suggested for helping accomplish this.

Suddenly the task of incorporating sheltered instruction into his lesson plans seemed overwhelming. If Mr. T. did all this, would he still have the time to make other needed modifications for his students? Where would he gain access to all the needed tools to implement this new approach?

QUESTIONS FOR REFLECTION

1. Although Mr. T. has a desire to implement this instructional strategy, will the benefits outweigh the required time commitment? Why or why not? (CC6S2)
2. In what ways are effective strategies to teach English language learners and students with disabilities the same? In what ways are they different? (CC6S2)

Whose Language Barrier?

Ms. Cox finished her IEP meeting with the Dumas family with that same old sense of guilt she felt after every meeting with them. The school translator was a nice addition to the IEP team but Ms. Cox felt some distance from the family because everything said between them had to go through the translator. She felt much closer to the families with whom she could converse directly. She had a personal goal to learn to speak Farsi for many years, as many of her students' families and people in her community spoke that as their primary language. Somehow that goal had never been achieved. She knew she had good intentions, but Ms. Cox wondered what was behind her delay in learning to speak fluent Farsi. The delay didn't fit with her overall goal of developing partnerships with the parents of her students.

Ms. Cox felt she had done a great job of developing partnerships with the parents of her students. She made home visits to all of her students' homes at the beginning of the school year. She held IEP preparation meetings with the parents of her students so she could ensure that their wishes and dreams were reflected on the IEPs and so that they weren't surprised by anything they heard at the official IEP meeting. She sent home notes almost every day, telling parents about their children's accomplishments. All the parents had her email address and her phone number, and she often communicated with the parents through email or over the phone so they could share successes and problem solve through any difficulties she faced or the family faced. For the parents who didn't speak English, all of this didn't work quite as well as Ms. Cox hoped. Overall, Ms. Cox had to say she was proud of the partnerships she had developed and felt they reflected what she had read about in the literature in terms of effective practice. So why hadn't she achieved that goal of learning to speak Farsi?

Learning Farsi wasn't the only goal Ms. Cox hadn't achieved, but she knew it was the one that caused her the most discomfort. She also knew that her limited ability in speaking Farsi wasn't the only language barrier she faced. Although the majority of her students spoke English or Farsi, almost every year she had another language represented. Recently, a growing number of her students' families spoke Spanish, Tagalog, or Khmer. How could she learn all those languages? She was lucky to have had several bilingual aides over the years who helped her communicate with the families and build on the primary language abilities of her students, but still, she felt more distance from the families with whom she could not converse directly. What could she do about this dilemma?

QUESTIONS FOR REFLECTION

1. What suggestions would you give to Ms. Cox in regard to the language barriers she faces? (CC6K2)
2. What strategies can be used to build partnerships with families who speak a language different from the primary language of their child's teacher? (CC6K3)

Bridging Language Barriers

Jazmine Sanchez arrived in kindergarten with a limited amount of expressive language in Spanish, which was understood only by those who knew her, and an even more delayed amount of English acquisition. Her kindergarten teachers were worried about the lack of progress she was making. Most importantly, they were concerned about her lack of attention. Jazmine failed two hearing tests administered by the school nurse, but the poor results were attributed to her current cold. By November, her teachers were able to convince Mrs. Sanchez to have a doctor examine Jazmine's hearing. It was then discovered that Jazmine had a severe hearing impairment in both ears.

Over the next five years, the school tried to provide supports to the family related to Jazmine's hearing issues, but the family continually refused those supports. It took a year for the IEP team to convince Jazmine's parents that speech therapy would be helpful and two years for them to be convinced that she would be helped by the school resource teacher. By third grade, the IEP team recommended the use of an FM system to help Jazmine hear what her teacher was saying. Her parents refused this support. Her parents felt she was making progress and that this FM system would stigmatize Jazmine more than was necessary.

For fourth grade, Jazmine was placed with a native Spanish-speaking teacher. This teacher's bilingual abilities had helped her develop great partnerships with the parents of students in her class, so the school team decided she would be a great teacher for Jazmine. As Jazmine's parents developed a relationship with the teacher, the teacher was able to help them share their fears, disappointments, and concerns about raising a child who had a hearing impairment. The teacher began offering suggestions to the parents and then came to the IEP meeting to share more strategies. At this IEP meeting, the FM system was discussed again.

Following one of these IEP meetings, Jazmine's fourth-grade teacher told the special education resource teacher that Jazmine's parents had told her they were very disappointed that the FM system had not been brought up at earlier IEP meetings. The resource teacher threw up her hands in frustration. She told Jazmine's fourth-grade teacher that they had discussed this at previous meetings and wondered why the parents didn't remember. After the fourth-grade teacher and resource teacher spoke some more, they realized that there had been a communication barrier. They spoke more with Jazmine's parents and discovered that terms used during previous meetings had not been translated clearly for the parents. Some terms were just confusing. Other terms were insulting to the parents and some were frightening. Jazmine had been described as "deaf" at meetings when the parents knew she had some hearing. The team discovered that the parents were embarrassed to ask questions at the meetings and that they didn't have supports to help them deal with their feelings. Once these things were discovered, the IEP team was able to develop a plan to bridge this language barrier. They began spending as much time planning for translation and clarifying translation at meetings as they did into actually writing Jazmine's IEP.

1. How does a team plan for effective translation? What preplanning and training is needed? (CC6K2)
2. What could the team have done early on to be more responsive to this family's language issues? (CC6K3)
3. What additional augmentative or assistive communication strategies should this team consider? (CC6K4)

What Have I Gotten Myself Into?

BY ROBERT MARKEL

Mr. Folger is in his third year of teaching and has decided to switch grade levels from sixth through eighth grades to fourth and fifth grades. He is excited about the change, and from his previous experience as a substitute teacher, he thinks that the fourth- and fifth-grade students are a good fit for him. When he first meets his students, Mr. Folger thinks to himself, "Yes, I made the right decision." His first day goes very well and he finds the students becoming actively engaged in the teaching and learning process. He likes all of his students and the paraprofessionals working with him are great. During the last 15 minutes before the students go home, Mr. Folger receives a note from the principal asking him to see her in her office after school. He begins to get a little nervous as he always does when he has to meet the principal and wonders what this is all about.

After school, Mr. Folger goes to the office to inquire about the note. The principal asks him if he would like to teach one English language development class. The principal explains that all students at the school are grouped by English language ability levels for a few hours each week and the teachers each instruct one of these groups. Mr. Folger quickly says that it would be his pleasure, since it sounds like the kind of schoolwide collaboration effort in which he has wanted to participate. Later that night, however, he begins to think about the situation. He asks himself several questions: "I have never taught an English language development program before. How will I do it? I've had one course on this topic and it's been addressed in several other classes, but I don't really know what I'm supposed to do. How is this different from what I do for effective special education instruction? What have I gotten myself into?"

QUESTIONS FOR REFLECTION

1. What are some of the similarities and differences between English language development models and effective special education models? (CC6S2)
2. What are some of the cultural and linguistic factors that Mr. Folger should take into consideration when he works with the students who are learning English as their second language? How can he be responsive to cultural mismatches between his use of English and that of his students learning the language? (CC6K2, CC6K3)

Labeling Dilemma

BY AMY LARSEN

At Diana's recent IEP meeting, the speech and language pathologist raved about Diana's amazing progress after three years of therapy. She announced that Diana no longer had a speech and language impairment in English or Khmer. The speech and language pathologist thought any remaining language concerns for 8-year-old Diana were a result of her limited knowledge of English, which could be addressed in her special education class. According to Diana's most recent psychoeducational evaluation, her eligibility label for special education services was a speech and language impairment that was determined to adversely affect her academic learning. Now that it was decided that she no longer had a speech and language impairment, the team was puzzled about what to do with her placement in the special education class.

The special education teacher shared that Diana was approximately three grade levels behind her same-age peers in all academic areas. The special education administrator, the school psychologist, and the general education teacher at the IEP meeting all felt that due to this delay, it wasn't in Diana's best interests to be placed in a general education classroom. They feared she would drown in the academics and not be able to keep up with her peers, even with modifications and accommodations. The psychologist said that the team therefore needed to diagnose a disability so they could keep her in her self-contained special education class placement.

QUESTIONS FOR REFLECTION

1. How can a disability be distinguished from a lack of knowledge of the English language? What are the legal implications under IDEIA of making a distinction between "language impairments" and "linguistic differences"? (CC6K1)
2. What impact might Diana's language delay have on her participation in general education? Would this be a sufficient reason to place her in a self-contained special education class? (CC652)

"Toilet, Water Closet, Baño . . ."

....

BY JOYCE SU

The importance of an effective communication system is something that shouldn't be taken for granted. Similarly, nothing can be more frustrating than when language barriers thwart the act of communication.

During the summer of Mrs. Ahmadinejad's first year of teaching, she was assigned to support a group of students with autism. It was a new experience for her because during the traditional school year, she was a resource teacher and the majority of her students had mild learning disabilities. Needless to say, Mrs. Ahmadinejad felt ill-prepared.

Out of the seven students in the summer school program, only two produced coherent verbal speech. The others were nonverbal or had difficulty producing comprehensible speech. They mostly used sounds or gestures (pulling the teacher's arm, pointing to pictures, screaming, etc.) to communicate.

One day, Oscar, age 9, took off running the other direction as the class returned from P.E. Assuming he was trying to escape from the activities awaiting him in the classroom, since his records said he was a "runner," Mrs. Ahmadinejan ran after him and tried to convince him to come back to class. He pushed her aside and continued running. She caught up with him only to discover that his destination was the water fountain. He took a drink and then immediately came back to where she was standing, and guilt overtook her. He was just thirsty, but he didn't have a communication system in place to communicate that to her.

The following week, a similar episode occurred. As the class was returning from lunch, Oscar tugged on Mrs. Ahmadinejan's arm when they reached the classroom door. She tugged him the opposite direction toward the classroom. He began to scream and pull away from her. When she let go, he ran off in the opposite direction. One of the aides volunteered to chase after him. Minutes later, both returned. The aide announced, "He had to use the bathroom." Instantly, a wave of guilt again flooded over Mrs. Ahmadinejad, and worsened as Oscar walked over toward her, smiling and guiding her in the direction of the board. He walked up to the board where she had put a picture schedule. He pointed to the picture of a toilet with the word *bathroom* written on top. It was as if he was trying to say, "I just had to use the bathroom. I wasn't trying to run away or misbehave." Tears welled up in her eyes as she apologized to Oscar.

That's twice she misread his actions and inaccurately guessed his intentions. How frustrating it must have been for him! After those two experiences, Mrs. Ahmadinejad felt determined to find some way for Oscar to conveniently communicate his needs, in a language both of them would understand. She also wondered why he did not bring a communication system with him to school or why no one had told her how to develop one.

QUESTIONS FOR REFLECTION

1. What augmentative and assistive communication strategies should this teacher consider implementing? (CC6K4)
2. How can teachers be sure students have the means necessary to communicate important messages even if they don't have verbal speech or an existing augmentative communication system? (CC6S1)

Twin Talk

BY KIM UFHOLTZ

Ahmed and Ara are identical twins. Both boys have severe articulation difficulties that have significantly impaired their ability to develop oral language. As a result, their interpersonal communication skills among peers and staff has been hampered. Ahmed and Ara use "twin talk" that is often unintelligible to others, which further delays the development of useful oral language. Because Ahmed and Ara are always together, Mr. Hall has noticed that both boys are becoming more isolated from their peers, especially during small groups and on the playground. After conferring with the speech and language pathologist, Mr. Hall feels something needs to be done to encourage language development and eliminate "twin talk."

QUESTIONS FOR REFLECTION

1. How have Ahmed and Ara's linguistic differences affected their growth and development? (CC6K1)
2. How might Mr. Hall select, design, or use technology that would help Ahmed and Ara communicate more effectively with peers and adults in the classroom and on the playground? What kinds of devices and vocabulary might be most appropriate? (CC6K4, CC6S1)

Who Speaks for Joey?

BY CAYCE CALDER

Joey is a fifth-grade student with a primary eligibility for special education under the categories of speech and language impairment and specific learning disability. Although Joey is able to speak, read, and communicate in English, he seems to be in a state of learned helplessness. Throughout Joey's life, his family and friends have spoken for Joey, causing him to rely on others for communication.

During class, it is typical for the teacher to ask a question of the whole group and have Joey raise his hand. When asked for the answer, Joey will scratch his chin, mumble quietly, and then say in a loud voice, "I forgot" or "Never mind." Someone will usually come to the rescue and answer the question for Joey. In turn, Joey will then say, "Yeah, yeah, that's what I meant!"

Joey is working below grade level in all subject areas. He tries hard every day, and math is his strongest subject. When assessing Joey in different areas, extra time is needed for him to complete his work. Overall, he seems to approach his daily routine in a passive manner, and his school team wants to figure out how to help him learn to take initiative in communication and learning.

QUESTIONS FOR REFLECTION

1. To what extent might the communication patterns practiced outside school contribute to Joey's limited class participation? How would you separate that from the impact of his speech and language impairment? Why would it be important to do this? (CC6K3)
2. Discuss the impact Joey's speech impairment appears to have had on his academic success. What strategies might the classroom teacher incorporate to help him address these areas of need? (CC6K1)

Lost in Translation

BY AMY LARSEN

Mahmoud always loved school and usually performed at grade average. He had lived in the United States for five years and spoke English fluently. During his third-grade year, Mahmoud was bused to a new school site where he was a student in Mr. Martin's third-grade general education classroom. He quickly made friends at his new school.

Initially, Mr. Martin did not notice Mahmoud standing out as a student who had difficulty learning. As the school year progressed, however, Mr. Martin became more and more concerned that Mahmoud seldom completed assignments and frequently asked for extra help in all subject areas.

Mr. Martin eventually consulted the prereferral team about Mahmoud's academic problems. As time went on, Mr. Martin truly believed that Mahmoud needed special education support because he could not keep up with his classmates. The prereferral team provided Mr. Martin with extra instructional strategies to help Mahmoud. They suggested breaking down assignments into smaller sections, providing outlines for class lectures, and preteaching essential vocabulary. They also shared with Mr. Martin some teaching methods using multiple modalities, such as giving both visual and oral directions and using art and drama. Mr. Martin said he would try those strategies, but he soon found they didn't really solve the problem. He referred Mahmoud again for testing to see if he was eligible for special education support because he really felt that both he and Mahmoud needed some extra help.

Mr. Martin tried to communicate with Mahmoud's parents but experienced great difficulty because they did not speak or read English well. Mahmoud and his brothers did the translating for them. When they met in person, Mr. Martin always felt like Mahmoud's parents seemed very formal and somewhat nervous and not too responsive to Mr. Martin's attempts to put them at ease. Mr. Martin felt frustrated by the lack of communication.

*Q*UESTIONS FOR REFLECTION

1. Identify some of the possible communication barriers that exist between Mr. Martin and Mahmoud and his family and identify strategies to overcome these barriers. (CC6K3)
2. How might cultural factors account for Mahmoud's parents' formal style of interacting with Mr. Martin and the limited effectiveness of his attempts to put them at ease? (CC6K2)

CHAPTER EIGHT

....

Instructional Planning

*T*he vignettes in this chapter reflect CEC Standard 7 as they provide examples of some of the issues teachers face as they plan instruction to fit each of their student's individual strengths and needs. They demonstrate how effective teachers develop long-range and short-range instructional programs to assist students in developing competencies in both general education and special education curricula. The vignettes also provide examples of the collaborative efforts necessary to develop and deliver instructional plans and to guide individualized transitions.

Selected Common Core Standards: #7 Instructional Planning

CC7K1   Theories and research that form the basis of curriculum development and instructional practice

CC7S1   Identification and prioritization of areas of the general curriculum and accommodations for individuals with exceptional learning needs.

CC7S2   Development and implementation of comprehensive, longitudinal individualized programs in collaboration with team members

CC7S8   Development and selection of instructional content, resources, and strategies that respond to cultural, linguistic, and gender differences

CC7S11   Preparation and organization of materials to implement daily lesson plans

No Supplies for Mr. Kennedy

BY JOY DYE

A week before a new school year was to begin, Mr. Kennedy received a phone call from his special education supervisor. The phone conversation revealed that Mr. Kennedy was going to have to make a change this year. Evidently, some families moved out of the district over the summer, which left Mr. Kennedy's fourth- and fifth-grade classrooms with a very low caseload. The supervisor informed Mr. Kennedy that the students he had last year were all being placed at other schools and that he would now be supporting kindergarten and first-grade students with mild/moderate disabilities.

After meeting his new principal, Mr. Kennedy was shown to his new resource room. He spent the whole day taking inventory of what he had to work with to help him plan instruction for his students. To his surprise, he found that there were no sets of kindergarten/first grade core curriculum in the bookshelves. Instead, he found outdated language arts teacher's editions in a variety of grade levels. A few outdated reading texts (not enough for the students on his caseload), some phonics workbooks, a few outdated math workbooks (again, not enough), some art supplies, plenty of records, a record player, and math manipulatives. He knew that he needed the appropriate core curriculum materials if he was going to be successful in planning instruction for the students on his caseload.

Mr. Kennedy approached the principal and requested to have a set of age-appropriate core curriculum materials to help him in planning. He was told to check the textbook room and that he could have anything that was there. He found appropriate science and social studies books, but no language arts texts or math workbooks. He returned to the principal and explained that he still needed language arts texts and math workbooks, and asked who to see about ordering them for his class. The principal's response to his request shocked Mr. Kennedy. The principal simply stated that most of his students will find that the language arts texts and math workbooks would be too hard for them, and that Mr. Kennedy should use the other resources that the previous teacher left in the room for him to use to teach reading and math. He asked the general education teachers if they had any textbooks to share with him and they said they had barely enough for each of the students in their classrooms.

Mr. Kennedy could not believe what he was hearing. How could he plan instruction for the students on his caseload if he didn't have access to the core curriculum materials they were expected to learn?

QUESTIONS FOR REFLECTION

1. What could Mr. Kennedy do to try to get the core curriculum materials? What does the law say about having access to the core curriculum materials? (CC7S2, CC7K2)
2. How can Mr. Kennedy go about utilizing the resources that he does have? (CC7S11)

Mrs. Banks, the special education support teacher, was nervous and excited. She had figured out how to match up the students with severe disabilities on her caseload with appropriate general education teachers for the coming year. She had thought a lot about student needs and abilities and each teacher's planning and instructional style, hoping to find a good fit. She thought she was now ready to submit this list to the planning team at the school site.

She knew that Andrew would fit well with Mrs. E. because both of them were very organized and liked things to be "just so." Nathan would fit well with Mrs. Watson because her class was very active, and even though the class sometimes seemed a little disorganized, Mrs. Banks had been in the classroom enough to see lots of good teaching and learning occur. The active and somewhat disorganized class would work well for Nathan because although he needed structure to follow a day's routine, he could handle a little disorganization, and also he needed to move around frequently. Mrs. Banks knew that Tristan, Nathan's friend, was also going to be in Mrs. Watson's class and somehow Tristan knew just how to help Nathan stay focused on what he needed to do. From observing the two boys together over the past year, Mrs. Banks knew Tristan could provide help to Nathan without negatively impacting his own school work. Jamie would do well with Mrs. Phillips because Mrs. Phillips was one of those really nice and soft-spoken teachers, and since Jamie got very agitated when people spoke to her sharply, Mrs. Phillips would be a good match for her. When she finished matching up all the other students, Mrs. Banks sat back and excitedly said aloud, "This could work!" Now, she needed to write an IEP summary and identify general information about appropriate individualized adaptations for each teacher and her student match as she had promised. She would then take this to the planning team.

QUESTIONS FOR REFLECTION

1. How does the decision making that Mrs. Banks engaged in demonstrate effective development of individualized programs involving collaboration of team members? (CC7S2)
2. What are some of the cultural, linguistic, and gender differences that Mrs. Banks might have considered as she matched her students with general education teachers? (CC7S8)

Planning for Mark

Kelly and Linda enjoy their co-teaching relationship. They work together to deliver language arts to Kelly's first-period class of sixth-graders. Linda, a special education teacher, remembered when she used to teach her students in her own separate special education classroom. She modified the grade-level standards and curriculum to meet her students' needs. Kelly, a sixth-grade teacher, remembered when she wasn't expected to teach students with disabilities in her classroom. They both saw the benefits of this new approach but found themselves sometimes relying on old habits as well.

Linda and Kelly meet once a week during their planning period to prepare for class and to evaluate student progress. They use a planning tool called the Planning Pyramid (Schumm, Vaughn, & Harris, 1997)—a framework for planning for diverse student needs. Linda and Kelly are using this tool to plan for daily lessons and have found it to be a successful way of identifying what *all* students will learn, what *most* students will learn, and what *some* students will learn.

Mark is one of their students who has significant delays in expressive and receptive language. Although Mark has been meeting some of his language goals in Kelly's class, his academic progress has been minimal. Linda and Kelly find it challenging to plan for the significantly modified curriculum Mark requires.

When using the Planning Pyramid, the teachers discovered that they plan for the base of the pyramid, or what *all* students will learn, with Mark's specific basic skill needs in mind. The remaining needed skills are then tailored to the rest of the students' abilities. This system seemed to be working great, but one glaring problem arose. Linda and Kelly found themselves satisfied with Mark's minimal progress on any day's lesson, but they are concerned that their current system of planning is actually lowering their expectations for Mark. The co-teachers found that they only expect Mark to master the most basic skill that they've identified for *all* students to learn. They feel they forget sometimes that he could rise above the most basic level of the pyramid.

QUESTIONS FOR REFLECTION

1. Identify challenges teachers might face in using this popular planning tool and others for students with diverse learning needs. (CC7K1, CC7S1)
2. What evidence of best practices for instructional planning can be identified in this vignette? (CC7S11)
3. How might these two teachers modify their current planning practices to ensure that the expectations for Mark aren't limited to very basic skills in each lesson? (CC7S2)

I Did It!

Mrs. Maldern sat back and thought, "I did it!"

Weeks ago Mrs. Maldern decided that her existing system of planning and tracking IEP goals was inefficient. She spent hours researching and planning a more efficient approach. The initial time required to establish this new system would be extensive, but Mrs. Maldern was sure the payoff would be more than beneficial in the long run.

She began by planning and delivering the needed assessments in reading and math. Using those data, Mrs. Maldern created small groups based on each student's ability levels. Although the small groups were able to target the students' needs in math and reading, there were still many individualized goals set forth in each IEP that needed to be addressed.

Mrs. Maldern then created a cross-matrix of every student's goals. She listed the students' names down the side and a brief statement of the year's goal across the top. She grouped these goals by targeted area. Mrs. Maldern then used this matrix when planning each lesson she would deliver in the small groups. She found that this type of planning allowed her to create lessons that targeted goals that were closely related. Additionally, the matrix was an excellent tool for tracking when she had worked on specific goals. Mrs. Maldern now felt that her instruction would be more effective and her planning would reflect better time management.

QUESTIONS FOR REFLECTION

1. What resources could Mrs. Maldern have used when researching and planning her new system? (CC7K1)
2. What other approaches could Mrs. Maldern use for lesson preparation in order to be sure she was addressing each individual student's IEP objectives? (CC7S10)
3. What might still be missing from Mrs. Maldern's instructional time that could make it more effective? (CC7S12)

How Will I Do It?

BY AMY LARSEN

Mr. Ecks was thinking of leaving teaching. He had too much to do in his special education resource teacher position. Wood shop, algebra, Spanish, physical education, social studies, health, home economics, American literature, calculus, and the list of general classes go on and on! Periods 1 through 7, 8:00 a.m. until 3:30 p.m., before- and after-school activities, lunch, passing periods, and so many students to support. He had 30 students on his caseload, each with five to seven learning goals. That meant he had to make plans to meet over 200 IEP goals, which meant many dozens of accommodations, modifications, and adaptations to implement all throughout the school day at Marina High School.

He needed to support Jose, Martha, Jennifer, Scott, Jason, Michael, Kim, Tameka, Kory, and so many more students at the same time and had only one paraprofessional to help him. Mr. Ecks felt entirely overwhelmed and didn't know how to fulfill his legal, ethical, and moral responsibilities to support these students. Not only did he want to develop appropriate plans to support his students but he also wanted to continue building positive relationships with the school staff. Additionally, he wanted to provide regular progress reports to the students' parents and get their input on any changes that needed to be made in his instructional planning. He just didn't know how he was going to do all this.

*Q*UESTIONS FOR REFLECTION

1. How can Mr. Ecks support all his students as stated on their IEPs on a daily basis? What are ways Mr. Ecks can collaborate with others so as to balance the many demands he has across the core curriculum areas for the many individuals he must support? (CC7S12)
2. What instructional strategies could Mr. Ecks implement to support all his students? (CC7S8)

Is This Okay?

Mrs. Smith has been newly hired as a special education resource teacher at an elementary school. The former teacher used a pull-out model for service delivery. Mrs. Smith planned to implement a collaborative, co-teaching approach. She knew that she would need to establish a good rapport with the teachers and to collaborate closely with the staff to achieve this goal, especially since the teachers at her school were used to the pull-out model.

She began by working with the upper-grade-level teachers. Most of her students were in grades 4 through 6. Over the course of the year, Mrs. Smith established a great working relationship with the fifth-grade teacher, Ms. Ikeda. Ms. Ikeda was an experienced, highly effective, and engaging teacher. She considered the learning needs of all her students and was willing to make needed adjustments in her expectations for individual students.

The opportunity finally arrived for Mrs. Smith to include 8 out of the 30 students on her caseload in a cluster in Ms. Ikeda's fifth-grade classroom. Ms. Ikeda had 20 other students in the class already. The teachers both thought that since there would be two teachers, they could successfully teach 28 students. When the time came to plan, the two teachers agreed on a co-teaching approach. Mrs. Smith would deliver the mathematics lessons and Ms. Ikeda would deliver the language arts program. They agreed to meet on a weekly basis and discuss how things were progressing. Both teachers recognized the benefits of such a service delivery model. But, as expected, challenges in this type of clustering existed as well. Sometimes it seemed like they were having to make too many accommodations, and behavior problems sometimes seemed to be more than one would typically expect. Concerned about the effectiveness of this model, Mrs. Smith wondered, "Is this okay?"

QUESTIONS FOR REFLECTION

1. What are some suggestions for Mrs. Smith and Ms. Ikeda when prioritizing areas of the general curriculum and accommodations for all students in this fifth-grade class? (CC7S1)

2. What are the benefits and limitations for planning individualized instruction when students with disabilities are clustered in big groups in general education classrooms? What are some of the factors these teachers should consider as they develop comprehensive individualized programs for all of the students? (CC7S2)

How Many Grade Levels?

BY AMY LARSEN

When people hear that Mrs. Garza is a teacher, they always ask what grade she teaches. She tells them, "I teach first grade, second grade, and third grade," which leads to quizzical expressions from the questioners.

All of Mrs. Garza's students have a labeled disability and differ widely in cognitive abilities. She loves the diversity of abilities, but she does struggle teaching all of them. It feels like a monumental task to teach three different grade levels of material day after day. Reading and language arts are her favorite subjects and she just received the materials for a new scripted program, *Open Court*, that the district has adopted for teaching in this area.

Now all she has to do is figure out the logistics of teaching all the first-, second-, and third-graders using the three different levels of the reading program. The teaching strategies and activities in *Open Court* are very effective, but Mrs. Garza just cannot figure out how to teach all the students. The scripted activities take many hours to complete each day. She can't imagine how she will do this and teach all the other subjects her students are supposed to be learning. It seems impossible to plan the school day the way she thinks she is supposed to.

*Q*UESTIONS FOR REFLECTION

1. How can Mrs. Garza plan instruction to manage the scope and sequence of the three grade levels? (CC7K2, CC7S1)
2. What are some strategies for preparing and organizing materials to implement daily lesson plans that incorporate multiple scripted programs? (CC7S11)
3. Are there any other considerations for ensuring the school's access to its state-adopted, grade-level curriculum? (CC7K3)

Teaching Addition

Turning on the overhead projector, Mr. Peck wrote the problem $48 + 76 = $ _____. "We're going to continue working on addition," he told his second-grade class. "Today I'm going to teach you about adding two-digit numbers."

Mr. Peck looked out over his 20 students. He noticed that Ryan was staring out the window, appearing to not be engaged in the lesson. Ryan's IEP stipulated a goal that had him working on one-to-one correspondence, and so Mr. Peck thought to himself that he had better be sure to incorporate this goal in the activity.

Shaking his head over what to do to engage Ryan, Mr. Peck's eyes then rested on Julia. Having just transferred into his class from another district, initial assessments were still being completed to determine her present levels of performance. So far, Mr. Peck had discovered that she didn't know her basic math facts.

Thinking about Julia, Mr. Peck's mind quickly flashed to Miguel. How much of this lesson would he understand, given his limited English proficiency? Miguel was still learning to count in English.

Already frustrated, and only one minute into the math lesson, Mr. Peck went back to instructing his class as he had planned. During the guided practice portion of this lesson, Mr. Peck passed out counting chips to Julia and Ryan. He quickly paired Miguel with another student to give him a model to follow. Writing the next problem on the overhead, "$44 + 98 = $ _____," Mr. Peck guided his class through the steps of finding the sum for these two-digit numbers. The special education teacher had provided Mr. Peck with materials from the kindergarten curriculum, so a page had already been photocopied for Ryan to complete during the students' independent practice. Mr. Peck assumed it would be best to just let Miguel and Julia attempt the second-grade work without any additional supports. He hoped the steps he had taken earlier in the lesson would allow these students some success on the assignment.

When math instruction ended for the day, Mr. Peck wasn't sure how well the lesson had gone. He had collected the second-grade work from his students and immediately noticed that Julia had missed a majority of the problems on the page. The alternative sheet he'd selected for Ryan was only partially completed. Concerned that his attempts at differentiated instruction were not working, Mr. Peck wondered what to do with tomorrow's lesson.

*Q*UESTIONS FOR REFLECTION

1. What are some effective tools Mr. Peck could have used for planning differentiated instruction? (CC7S10)
2. What should a teacher look for to make responsive adjustments to instruction based on continual observations? (CC7S13)

CHAPTER NINE

....

Assessment

*T*he vignettes in this chapter relate to CEC Standard 8 as they provide examples of some of the issues teachers face as they assess for program planning as well as for ongoing monitoring and evaluation. They demonstrate how effective teachers apply their knowledge of the legal and ethical principles of measurement as they assess the individual needs and abilities of their students. The vignettes also demonstrate how effective teachers collaborate with others to employ nonbiased and meaningful assessments and use the results of these assessments to identify supports and adaptations that will fit student needs and to monitor student progress.

Selected Common Core Standards: #8 Assessment

CC8K4   Use and limitations of assessment instruments

CC8S4   Development or modification of individualized assessment strategies

CC8S5   Interpretation of information from formal and informal assessments

CC8S7   Assessment results reported to all stakeholders using effective communication skills

CC8S8   Evaluation of instruction and monitoring of progress of individuals with exceptional learning needs

How to Test?

BY JOY DYE

Mrs. Petrillo is close to finishing her first year of supporting first- through third-grade students identified as having mild to moderate disabilities. She only has one more triennial reevaluation left for her student, Jason. She is glad that Jason's triennial was late in the year, because it took her almost the whole school year to understand Jason's behavior and how best to deal with it. Jason cannot adapt easily to changes in his environment. Whether it be a new student, a change in the routine schedule, a change in the weather, or even a new piece of jewelry someone wore, it would seem to set Jason off. He would scratch, spit, and cry out loud if a certain change would occur.

Throughout the year, Mrs. Petrillo learned how to help Jason when he got upset. She learned how to prepare him for a change in the schedule by giving him advanced warnings and gently walking him through the change. She provided a gentle hand on his shoulder when anyone new came into the class. If the weather was windy, she would let the students play inside the classroom during recess time. Also, Mrs. Petrillo was very careful about choosing what jewelry she would wear each day. However, she was a bit nervous when thinking about having to complete a required formal standardized test on Jason. She gave herself a whole month to complete the testing, knowing that it was not going to be easy.

Mrs. Petrillo chose to begin the testing on a day when Jason was in a very good mood and motivated to work. She asked Jason to come with her to the testing room she was required to use. Since she had built up a great deal of trust between herself and Jason, Mrs. Petrillo was able to lead Jason into the testing room with the testing materials laid out on the table and ready to use. Jason squeezed Mrs. Petrillo's hand tightly and began to tug her in the opposite way to leave the room. Mrs. Petrillo was able to coax Jason over to the table, but once seated and seeing all the materials on the table that were very different from what he was used to seeing, Jason began crying and backing away toward the door. Mrs. Petrillo was glad he didn't spit and scratch, as he might have in the past, but she also felt she couldn't test him when he was this upset. She could do nothing else but go back to the classroom and figure out another way to do this.

The next week, Mrs. Petrillo brought along another student for the testing session to see if this would put Jason at ease. Jason did participate more than he had in the past, but Mrs. Petrillo found she often had to change the wording on questions and vary response modes to keep Jason involved. She wondered if these changes invalidated his test scores, for she had been warned about this in her training for using this test. She also wondered if she was going to end up with any information that would meaningfully inform her decisions about Jason's educational programming. Was she just going through the motions because this testing was required?

$\mathcal{Q}$UESTIONS FOR REFLECTION

1. How do modifications teachers may make in administering a standardized test affect the validity of the test scores? (CC8S2)
2. Describe the limitation of using this type of standardized test. (CC8K4)
3. How can a teacher arrange a testing situation to help a student feel more comfortable? (CC8S9)

Are You Sure?

Mrs. Freeman had to laugh when she saw LaDawn and the new school psychologist return to her class. When the new school psychologist had talked about performing an assessment on LaDawn, Mrs. Freeman had suggested that the school psychologist might want to conduct the assessment in a familiar place. She explained that LaDawn was nonverbal and didn't react well to changes in her routine or unfamiliar places, but the school psychologist said that she had a room already set up for the assessment so they would just go there. The school psychologist came to pick up LaDawn a little later and they were gone from the class for about an hour. When they returned, LaDawn was skipping and laughing (something she rarely did), but the school psychologist looked exhausted and bedraggled. Mrs. Freeman asked what happened and the school psychologist said that LaDawn had not answered any questions or cooperated in any of the testing activities. The school psychologist said she had tried everything that she had learned in school to engage LaDawn in the activities but nothing seemed to work. Mrs. Freeman could tell the school psychologist was feeling very discouraged.

Mrs. Freeman asked the school psychologist if she wanted to meet to discuss this more after school and the school psychologist said that yes, she would. After school, the two women met in Mrs. Freeman's classroom. She asked the school psychologist what kind of information she wanted and the school psychologist said that she wanted to know if LaDawn could match colors. Mrs. Freeman replied yes, that LaDawn regularly matched colors when she helped put away math manipulatives and color-coded student folders. The school psychologist said she had tried to find out if LaDawn could match like items, and Mrs. Freeman said that LaDawn regularly did this when she helped clean up after lunch as she sorted trays, silverware, and cups. She showed the school psychologist data sheets to demonstrate LaDawns's regular performance on this task. The two women discussed the assessment topics for a good bit longer and found that there were many things that LaDawn did in her daily routine that she would not perform in the formal testing situation. At the end of their discussion, the school psychologist said that she now faced a dilemma. She had evidence that LaDawn could perform many of the tasks that were part of her assessment tool, but she did not do them during the testing session, meaning that the results might not be valid according to the assessment tools validated procedures. The two women wondered what to do.

QUESTIONS FOR REFLECTION

1. What limitations of the assessment instrument that the school psychologist used are reflected in this vignette? (CC8K4)
2. How might the assessment procedure be modified to meet the unique needs and abilities of LaDawn? What are the implications of modifying this assessment procedure? (CC8S9)

Finding a Way

BY KIM UFHOLTZ

Ms. Bedard works with special education students in kindergarten through second grade, most of whom have speech and language delays. A majority of her instruction is focused on encouraging oral language along with a focus on basic literacy skills.

The district mandates that teachers use benchmark assessments to determine individual performance. Scores are gathered through phonemic awareness assessments and reading benchmarks, which take a running record and ask comprehension questions. Both of these assessments are used as district criteria for promotion to the next grade level.

Ms. Bedard thinks that it is important that her students participate in grade-level assessments. She wants to assure their access to the core curriculum and have tools available to be accountable for student progress. At the same time, Ms. Bedard isn't sure if these assessments can be modified enough to appropriately measure her students' progress. Most of her students are unable to produce the oral language required by these assessments. In order to allow the students to participate, Ms. Bedard must find alternative ways to assess her students. Some students use augmentative communication devices, which would give her means to assess comprehension. But Ms. Bedard remains unsure if it is appropriate to use these assessment tools, and, if so, how.

QUESTIONS FOR REFLECTION

1. How could Ms. Bedard adapt and or modify the assessments to accommodate the unique abilities and needs of these individuals? (CC8S4)
2. Discuss the challenges and limitations of using curriculum assessment tools that assume a basic ability and skill level with students with disabilities. (CC8K4)

Going through the Motions

BY KIM MARTIN

Mrs. Michaels was in the middle of completing all her coursework to obtain her special education credential. Because there was a teacher shortage, she had been hired as a teacher even though she didn't yet have a credential. As the special education representative, she has just left Omar's initial IEP meeting and is feeling very frustrated. Omar has just been found eligible for special education support services and so this meeting was the first time for the team to get together to develop plans for him. Omar is 8 years old and hasn't yet passed the kindergarten benchmarks, and so everyone is concerned about him. Mrs. Michaels assessed Omar and wrote some IEP objectives but the IEP meeting was led by the school psychologist and school counselor. As Mrs. Michaels followed along with the meeting, she found that large parts of the IEP document were being only partially explained and others were not being explained at all. Mrs. Michaels attemped to explain some of the points in more detail but the meeting facilitators kept rushing the meeting along. Omar's mom appeared to be listening to the exchange and repeatedly said how thankful she was that Omar was finally getting some help. She signed the IEP but Mrs. Michaels wondered if Omar's mom really understood what was in the document. Mrs. Michaels is now uncertain of what to do but knows that she is very frustrated with how people at the meeting just seemed to be going through the motions.

*Q*UESTIONS FOR REFLECTION

1. What can Mrs. Michaels do to ensure that Omar's mother is meaningfully informed about all aspects of the IEP document she just signed? (CC8K1, CC8S7)
2. What should have happened before the IEP meeting to ensure that the meeting would be more informative for all participants? (CC8K3)

Meaningful Monitoring

BY JOY DYE

Mr. Lind was preparing for his parent report card conferences. This was his second year supporting junior high students with mild to moderate disabilities as their special education teacher. As he looked through his students' portfolios he had prepared for the conferences, he wished he could have something more than just work samples to show the parents. All of his students were working on different goals from their IEPs and Mr. Lind wanted to show the parents something more individualized that reflected their progress toward meeting their individual goals. Instead, the students' portfolio work samples were all very similar to one another, showing the students' progress in the general standardized education curriculum.

He wasn't sure how he could show the individualized growth of each of his students. Whenever a student had an annual or triennial meeting coming up, Mr. Lind would assess the student to see if the student had met his or her goal. Sometimes he would find that his students did indeed meet their goals, but at other times some students did not meet their goals. This would surprise Mr. Lind because he had thought that the students had been progressing and learning a great deal. He knew that he should change his current method of ongoing monitoring. The portfolios looked great, but they didn't always offer meaningful evidence on how the students were progressing toward their individual goals, since he was required to use certain artifacts for all of the students. How was he going to develop a monitoring system that gave him meaningful information and helped him make needed adjustments in curriculum and instruction? Was it going to require a lot more planning and time?

QUESTIONS FOR REFLECTION

1. What are some of the changes Mr. Lind can make in order to achieve his desire to have a more visual and accurate system of monitoring how his students are progressing toward their goals? (CC8S4)
2. Where should Mr. Lind start in developing his monitoring system? (CC810)

How Much Can I Do?

Mrs. Dean gathered up all the papers she had just been given at her district-level training on state-required alternative testing. Guidelines and instructions for administration had been carefully reviewed. Although she had used the alternative assessment created by her district in the past, the new state procedures were much more detailed. Mrs. Dean was happy to finally have the needed instructions on the legally required alternate testing.

Mrs. Dean had three students with moderate to severe disabilities who would be participating in this testing. The IEP team for each of these students had determined that instead of participating in standardized testing, the state alternate test would be a more appropriate assessment for these individuals. These three students were fully included in general education and would need to be tested during the same time period that her other students were taking the state-required standardized tests.

When it came time for Mrs. Dean to create a schedule of how to administer this test, she saw how many hours it would take to test each of these students individually. Because of the varying grade levels and ability levels of her students, each portion of the test would need to be delivered one-to-one. Some portions of the test could take 30 minutes or more to complete. Student cooperation and attention also needed to be figured into this schedule as well. In addition to the time demands of the alternate test, her other students required their state standardized test to be administered with the IEP-documented accommodations and modifications. How was she supposed to complete all this in the given two-week window? There didn't seem to be enough hours in the day. Mrs. Dean asked, "How much can I do?"

QUESTIONS FOR REFLECTION

1. What are the legal and ethical provisions that should guide an IEP team in determining if a student should participate in alternate assessments? (CC8K2)
2. With time being an obvious challenge, describe additional limitations of alternate assessment tools used in lieu of statewide standardized assessments. (CC8K4)
3. What are some suggestions for time management and administration of these assessments? (CC8S2)

Too Much Already!

Mr. Kane cringed when the Discrete Trial Therapy support provider arrived in his classroom. His school district had adopted a Discrete Trial Therapy support model for all students identified with disabilities. He knew that he would be asked for the data sheets that he was required to fill out, but he also knew that he had not been able to keep up with the intense data collection activities. Mr. Kane really did feel bad about this because he had been excited about collaborating with the Discrete Trial Therapy program staff, as he knew the parents felt this therapy had really helped their son, Tom. Mr. Kane had started to read more about Discrete Trial Therapy and found there were studies supporting this application of applied behavior analysis but there were also studies that questioned its effectiveness. Regardless of these questions, Mr. Kane really valued collaborating with other professionals, so this new form of collaboration seemed like a good way to learn new skills. However, the more he participated in this very structured therapy program, he found that it kept interfering with his other duties. His paraprofessionals really tried to keep on top of the data collection activities but often were pulled away by other obligations. He also knew Tom missed many class activities while he was engaged in the therapeutic activities. Mr. Kane knew the time had come to face up to these difficulties and figure out how he could infuse this very intense therapeutic model into his class.

*Q*UESTION FOR REFLECTION

1. What are some suggestions for teachers like Mr. Kane who are faced with overwhelming requirements for progress monitoring? (CC8S10, CC8S8)

Am I Cheating?

BY AMY LARSEN

The students Mrs. Thalia supports have mild and moderate disabilities. They are reading and applying reading strategies and skills to read new texts. The second- and third-graders are incredibly excited that they can actually read "real" books. These students love to take their books home and read them to their families and neighbors.

The students' present levels in reading range from reading pictures to what Mrs. Thalia's district considers a beginning second-grade reading level. The district has created a standard reading assessment that is to be administered as soon as the teacher feels students will successfully pass a specific reading passage. There are many problems with this district assessment. As a result, students are regularly mislabeled as a lower reader than teachers consider them to be. Mrs. Thalia's assessment of their reading level is based on day-in and day-out observation, student work, and ongoing data collection (e.g., running records), which she feels are more accurate and valid.

In Mrs. Thalia's district, many teachers think that the required reading assessments are invalid. Many of the words in the reading passages do not seem to match the level they are supposedly testing. Additionally, many of the reading assessment passages contain content many students may have not experienced personally. For example, one passage contains content about experiences with grandparents and another included the topic of "aquariums." Many of her students do not know their grandparents and others had never heard the word *aquarium,* so they found it difficult to relate to these reading selections. Consequently, Mrs. Thalia's students often failed to meet the district's criteria to pass these assessments.

Because of all the challenges with the district's standard reading assessment, Mrs. Thalia decided to change reading instruction. She specifically used many of the words from the reading assessment passages in her lessons. For example, words from the passages might appear in spelling lists or vocabulary walls. The selected vocabulary might be focused on in mini-lessons in guided reading groups, shared reading, read alouds, and word games.

Items around the classroom are labeled with words from these passages as well. For example, the fish tank in the classroom is labeled "aquarium" because this is one of the words found in a required text. Mrs. Thalia is trying to provide experiences that simulate content in the reading assessment to give her students prior knowledge and a better chance for success on the test. She wonders, however, if she is cheating by teaching to the test in this manner.

*Q*UESTIONS FOR REFLECTION

1. Do you think Mrs. Thalia is cheating by teaching the words on the assessement? (CC8K2)
2. Do these types of adaptations alter the results of this assessment? If so, would there be better ways of preparing students for the assessment criteria? (CC8S2)
3. Identify the limitation of this type of required assessment. (CC8K4)

....

CHAPTER TEN

Professional and Ethical Practices

T he vignettes in this chapter relate to CEC Standard 9 as they reflect the issues teachers encounter as they fulfill multiple roles and as they address the complex situations that teachers face on a daily basis. Effective teachers are reflective practitioners who are life-long learners who regularly engage in critical reflection on their practices with other professionals as well as the attitudes and beliefs that influence their decision making. This isn't always easy when teachers are faced with busy daily routines. Even with those busy daily lives, effective teachers appreciate the diversity of their students and their families and do their best to evidence ethical practices with respect for their own individual strengths and limitations.

Selected Common Core Standards: #10 Professional and Ethical Practices

CC9K4   Methods to remain current regarding research-validated practice

CC9S3   Ethical action when advocating for appropriate services

CC9S5   Demonstration of commitment to developing the highest education and quality-of-life potential of individuals with exceptional learning needs

CC9S7   Practice within one's skill limit and obtaining assistance as needed

CC9S11 Reflection on one's practice to improve instruction and guide professional growth

What Do I Ask For?

Mr. Mason is just starting out in his first year of teaching. He's still working on finishing the classes to complete his credential but the district said it would hire him before he was done, so that's how he finds himself here—balancing teaching, coursework, and his family. He's still learning the ropes in teaching but is pleased with the progress that the children in his special education class are making. He also finds himself losing sleep as he wonders why what he sees in his own school doesn't seem to fit with the practices he's hearing described in his college courses. He learned there that children have a right to be educated in the general education classes but some teachers at his school tell him, "We don't do that here" or "We don't do that with kids like yours." The principal says, "We can't rush these things," but Mr. Mason wonders who is rushing, since the law that promotes such inclusive models was passed more than 30 years ago.

It's not just including his kids in general education classes that Mr. Mason worries about. He wonders how best to help his students develop their comprehension skills. Sometimes they seem to understand the story he's read to them or the stories they read themselves but other times they don't seem to understand simple words. He knows his student Reynaldo often speaks to him in what is described as his primary language, Tagalog, but still isn't sure how much he understands in either Tagalog or English. He thinks some of the other students also speak languages other than English, but the records he was provided when he started his job weren't clear. He wishes he were bilingual but isn't sure how to fit building those skills into his already tight teaching and night school schedule. Mr. Mason asks the principal about this issue as well, and she says, "I'll check on what we can do about that." They had this discussion quite a while ago and so he asks others in the district what to do about it. They say, "I'll check on what we can do about that." He's now waiting for responses. He wonders, "How can I teach my students to comprehend what they are reading if I can't comprehend the language they understand?"

Mr. Mason worries about being a pest as well. Will he get in trouble for continually asking for more assistance for his students? He decides to ask another district support person, who replies, "You are right. We need to do something. Let's hire a bilingual aide for the class." Mr. Mason is ecstatic but also wonders will he always have to ask, ask, and ask again to get his students the help they need? Is that what he should do to help his students have increased opportunities to be educated in general education classrooms? He wonders, "Will I know what to ask for?"

*Q*UESTIONS FOR REFLECTION

1. What are the inherent problems involved in juggling coursework for initial teaching preparation with full-time teaching responsibilities and life outside of school and work? (CC9S7)
2. How should Mr. Mason respond the principal's notion that "we can't rush things" in regard to mainstreaming and inclusion? (CC9S3)
3. How should Mr. Mason handle his fear that he will have to ask, ask, and ask again to get his students the help they need? (CC9S8)

Where Is She?

....

BY KIM UFHOLTZ

Mrs. Jones has been a special education teacher supporting students with mild to moderate disabilities for several years. Most of her student population consists of second-language learners and fall into the lower socioeconomic status group. For the past two school years Mrs. Jones has been working with Anita, the program specialist, who is the person designated to act between class/school sites and the district office. Anita's role is to provide support to Mrs. Jones to meet some of the specific needs of her students and help coordinate services. Although Mrs. Jones realizes the program specialist has numerous responsibilities, her inability to reach Anita regarding student concerns or questions about an IEP has tested her patience. Mrs. Jones continues to make numerous phone calls with no response from Anita. On occasion, Mrs. Jones has asked her principal to email Anita with hopes of resolving matters or getting some sort of response, yet few messages are ever answered. Out of frustration, Mrs. Jones sometimes believes the lack of response may be because her students' issues or concerns may not take precedence over another school site. Where is Anita when Mrs. Jones needs help?

*Q*UESTIONS FOR REFLECTION
....

1. With the limited support that Mrs. Jones perceives she is receiving, how can she demonstrate a commitment to develop the highest education potential for her students? (CC9S5)
2. In upholding a high standard of competence and integrity for herself and for Anita, what would be the next step for Mrs. Jones to resolve this issue to obtain the assistance needed? (CC9S7)

Why Isn't Your Homework Done?

BY KIM MARTIN

Paul is a middle school student with a diagnosis of muscular dystrophy and his condition appears to be rapidly deteriorating. As part of the learning experience, students in Paul's class are expected to complete a weekly homework packet that is individualized for their particular skill level. Paul has never been very consistent in turning in that weekly homework. The homework is individualized for his skill level, and the task is designed to teach responsibility and independence. His teacher feels these are two skill areas on which Paul and his family should focus. Yet, at the same time, the teacher also recognizes that in light of Paul's limited life expectancy, his parents are giving other activities a higher priority than homework.

This problem isn't limited to just Paul, so his teacher decides to start increasing student homework completion by devising a plan that will reward students for completing their weekly homework. This seems like a logical way to get students motivated to bring in their homework. When Paul's family was advised that students who complete 95 percent of their homework packet would get to go off campus for lunch with the teacher, Paul began bringing in his homework. Now the classroom teacher wonders if students shouldn't just be motivated to do their homework because it's assigned.

Additionally, are his parents having Paul complete this homework just to allow him the social opportunity of off-campus lunch? She wonders what Paul's family may be giving up by focusing their attention on completing homework to earn lunch with the teacher. Was this push for homework completion as important as she thought?

QUESTIONS FOR REFLECTION

1. Is this homework approach beneficial to students in the long run? Is it beneficial to Paul in particular? (CC9S12)
2. How can Paul's teacher effectively deal with the ethical issues at play in this case? (CC9S1)

Setting Limits?

....

Ms. Low is tired again. She was up late. This time it was to take Jannice to the emergency room with her newborn baby. She knows her colleagues at school think she needs to do a better job of setting limits, but she also knows that if she doesn't take Jannice to the emergency room, the 13-year-old and her newborn baby may have no other way to get the medical help they need. She's tried getting Jannice connected with social service agencies but Jannice says the agencies all make her feel bad about having her baby. She loves her baby and is happy to have something of her own to take care of. Ms. Low knows the family tries to help Jannice but they are already stretched to the limit just trying to keep food on the table. Ms. Low has worked hard to make sure Jannice stays in school and doesn't want lack of acceptance from others to turn her away from school. So far, she's staying up with her school work and so Ms. Low wonders, "What is the right limit to set?"

As is the usual routine, when Ms. Low gets to school she finds Malika waiting by her door. She's working hard to keep Malika in school as well. She knows that Malika's assertiveness is something that will serve her well in life but also knows it tends to get her in trouble at school. Malika has sworn at teachers, used obscene gestures, and seems always to be in conflict with one teacher or another. Peers seem to respect her for her assertiveness but Ms. Low knows it's a balancing act trying to keep Malika's behavior within the limits of what the school views as acceptable without losing the voice and power that serve her well outside of school. She worries that Malika fits too closely the pattern described by O'Connor—that her assertiveness places her at risk for dropping out because of increasing conflict with school officials. Malika keeps her behavior in balance with Ms. Low. She doesn't lose the aggressiveness but she doesn't confront Ms. Low. "Why is that?" Ms. Low wonders. "Don't others respect the power and self-esteem that Malika so clearly evidences?" Again, her mind turns to the colleagues who tell her to set limits. Is allowing Malika to hang out in her class before school within limits?

How about the weekly home visit to Bonnie's house? Is that within limits? She knows that these weekly visits keep Bonnie's family connected with school. The parents just aren't comfortable coming to school but are extremely grateful for Ms. Low's visits when she shows them how to help Bonnie keep up with her homework. She's made great progress over the year but Ms. Low wonders, "Will her family get this kind of support when Bonnie heads to high school next year?" Other teachers say they wouldn't go near the neighborhood but Ms. Low has gotten to know the family and all the neighbors and wonders what those other teachers are talking about. "What are the limits on helping my students learn and stay in school?" Ms. Low wonders.

1. How would you respond to Ms. Low's reflection on "What are the limits on helping my students learn and stay in school?" (CC9S11)

2. What can Ms. Low do to advocate for Jannice and facilitate Jannice's connections with social service agencies? How can she serve as an advocate for Malika and assist her colleagues in accepting Malika's assertive behavior that serves her so well outside of school? (CC9S3)

3. What can schools do to facilitate partnerships with parents like Bonnie's parents who are uncomfortable coming to the school? (CC9S12)

The Loss of a Talented Teacher

BY ROBERT MARKEL

Mr. Lavine was a kindergarten teacher at Heartgrove School. He was one of those teachers who put his heart and soul into his teaching. He came to school each day with a smile on his face, ready to touch the lives of each of his students. Not only was he an excellent teacher but he was also an extremely talented artist. He used his talents to enhance his teaching practices and bring joy to the students.

Through the years, Mr. Lavine noticed that the standards for the school district were getting tougher and tougher for his students. One year, students were required to write a few three- to four-word sentences. In the years that followed, the students were required to write an entire story. Sure, some of the students could perform, but some students had never been in school before they came to Mr. Lavine's class. More importantly, Mr. Lavine felt that they had not yet developed the cognitive skills or fine motor skills needed for writing.

Toward the end of Mr. Lavine's eighth year as a teacher at Heartgrove School, his students spent less time learning how to be creative through such activities as interactive play, drawing, painting, and creating crafts. They also spent less time learning how to be kids. Mr. Lavine was spending all of his time in the classroom having the students try to write to prompts. He thought these prompts must have been created by adults at the district office who had not been in the classroom in years. Mr. Lavine wondered how he could recapture the joy for teaching that he felt in previous years.

*Q*UESTIONS FOR REFLECTION

1. How can a teacher support educational standards that seem to contradict best practices, as supported by research? (CC9K4)
2. How might Mr. Lavine's personal biases or different beliefs be affecting his teaching? (CC9K1)
3. What professional development activities might be appropriate for Mr. Lavine as he reflects on his professional responsibilities as a teacher? (CC9K3, CC9S9)

A New System

BY JOY DYE

Mrs. Davis supports 11 students with mild to moderate disabilities. She has just been informed at her monthly site meeting that Nick, a student from Mr. Armstrong's self-contained class for students with moderate to severe disabilities, might be joining Mrs. Davis during her reading and writing hour. Nick can read very quietly out loud when someone points to the words on the text. He can also repeat phrases that are spoken to him. He does not speak outside these two situations. Nick is able to answer questions about the reading by pointing to the correct answer. Currently, Nick is beginning to use a Picture Exchange Communication System (PECS) to express his ideas, needs, and wants as much as possible, but he is not quite independent in using this system. Usually the teacher or the paraeducator gives him prompts to help him communicate. Mrs. Davis is somewhat familiar with PECS, but doesn't feel she knows enough about it to teach reading and writing using PECS.

Mrs. Davis has a great system worked out to meet the needs of all her current students. Her students are clustered into three groups so that she and the paraeducator can rotate between the groups. This system took about a month to set up and to work out the flaws. Mrs. Davis's students are responding wonderfully and showing much improvement in their writing and reading. All of her students are verbal and able to express their ideas, needs, and questions. How will she meet Nick's needs, which seem so different from the needs of other students she supports? Will Nick's presence affect the progress of her other students?

QUESTIONS FOR REFLECTION

1. What needs to occur to help make this transition successful for Nick? (CC9S5)
2. What professional growth activities might Mrs. Davis need to gain the needed skills for working with Nick? (CC9S7, CC9S11)
3. Should assistive technology be brought up at the IEP meeting? What kinds of technology could help Mrs. Davis communicate to Nick more efficiently, or help Nick communicate to Mrs. Davis and the other students more efficiently? (CC9S10)

Should I Ask for Help?

BY JOY DYE

Jack is a first-grade student who started the school year obsessed with touching other students' hair, clothing, class work—pretty much anything his eyes became fixed on. This behavior clearly created a disturbance within the classroom. Miss Webb, Jack's teacher, tried verbal warnings and used her positive behavior system, but with no avail.

Miss Webb, a first-year teacher, shared this problem with her trusted colleague who had been a special education teacher for 15 years. The colleague suggested that Miss Webb allow Jack to hold a "squeeze ball" in his hands during rug time, group time, or whenever the need arose to keep Jack's hands busy. To Miss Webb's surprise, the ball worked. Jack's obsession with touching seemed to disappear.

Recently, however, Miss Webb has watched Jack begin a new behavior. He spits on his shoes, on his books, on his fingers, on the floor—it does not end. Miss Webb told Jack that she did not like spit in her classroom. Jack responded that he liked spit. Miss Webb tried focusing on Jack's positive behavior, rewarding Jack whenever he did not spit. She tried taking away recess time and using time-outs, but nothing seemed to be working. She even talked to her trusted colleague again, but her few suggestions were things Miss Webb had already tried.

Miss Webb consulted with the school psychologist, who suggested several different interventions that she tried, but they didn't work. When they didn't work, Miss Webb wondered if she was doing something wrong. She began to think that her inability to improve Jack's behavior might reflect negatively on her as a teacher. Should she ask for more help?

QUESTIONS FOR REFLECTION

1. What other resources could Miss Webb use to help her with Jack's behavior? (CC9K3, CC9K4)
2. What suggestions would you give this teacher about reacting to Jack's behaviors? (CC9S6)

Paperwork Overload

BY REBECCA DENNIS

Mr. and Mrs. Tacklind have always been advocates for their daughter Maya who has a learning disability. Therefore, when they saw that Maya had received an F on her report card for history, they phoned the special education resource teacher with a concern. They wanted to make sure that Maya had received the accommodations that her IEP outlined for her in the history class. The resource teacher asked the history teacher if Maya was given appropriate accommodations within her classroom. The history teacher said that Maya had indeed received such accommodations but the teacher had no proof or documentation of them. When the resource teacher told the history teacher that they would have to document accommodations made, she complained, stating, "I have too many students to worry about. How can I keep track of the things I do without adding more to my workload? Why don't you all just trust me?" The resource teacher wondered what kind of support she could give to help with documentation and to keep the parents informed about Maya's progress in history.

QUESTIONS FOR REFLECTION

1. How can teachers document accommodations without overloading on paperwork? Should teachers be held to a high standard of competency in this area? (CC9S2)
2. How might the special education resource program teacher support the history teacher? (CC9S11)

Why Are You Teaching?

BY REBECCA DENNIS

Debbie, a local college student, was working on her teaching credential in mathematics. One of the assignments in her Introduction to Working with Students with Exceptional Needs class was to observe in a special education classroom. She arranged an observation in a local elementary school that had a class for students with moderate to severe disabilities. Debbie was both excited and nervous about the observation because she had never been in a special education classroom and was curious to see how the teacher would modify the standards to teach this population of students.

When she entered Mrs. Martin's classroom, Debbie was taken aback. Most elementary classrooms she had been in were bright, organized, and colorful. This classroom was cluttered and lacked any personal touches or classroom decorations. Even the bulletin boards had the bare minimum posted on them—only the school bell schedule and a calendar. As Debbie found a place to sit and observe, she decided to reserve her personal judgments, since she realized that not everyone needs to decorate to be an effective teacher. However, as the observation continued, she wondered how the students were learning anything at all. Within the three-hour observation, the students were not taught much of anything. They began with a coloring activity, moved on to watching a video, and then sat around the classroom having "free time" before they prepared for lunch. During the entire observation Debbie noticed that the paraeducators took care of all the students' needs while the teacher sat at her desk first reading the newspaper then talking on the phone.

Although the students had severe disabilities, Debbie knew that they were capable of doing more than simply coloring; she wondered why there was no real curriculum being taught. She quietly asked a paraeducator if this was a special "free day" for the students. The paraeducator responded, "No, why?" As Debbie left the observation, she thought about all she had learned in her class about modifying the curriculum and inclusion and wondered why Mrs. Martin taught this class when it seemed liked she didn't care about providing effective, meaningful instruction. Why was Mrs. Martin "teaching"?

QUESTIONS FOR REFLECTION

1. What impact does this teacher's actions and attitudes have on the students and paraprofessionals in the class? (CC9K2)
2. If this one observation was in fact a good example of her typical approach to teaching, do you think Mrs. Martin's classroom management and teaching style violate the CEC Code of Ethics? (CC9S1)
3. How do you define "professional" behavior? (CC9S4)

CHAPTER ELEVEN

Collaboration

*T*he vignettes in this chapter relate to CEC Standard 10 as they provide examples of the necessary collaboration with families, other educators, related service personnel, and representatives from community agencies to effectively meet the needs of individuals with exceptional needs. They demonstrate cultural responsivity as well as the challenges teachers face as they advocate for their students and fulfill their function as "specialists" who serve as resources to their colleagues.

Selected CEC Common Core Standards: #10 Collaboration

CC10K2   Roles of individuals with exceptional learning needs, families, and school and community personnel in the planning of an individualized program

CC10K3   Concerns of families of individuals with exceptional learning needs and strategies to help address these concerns

CC10K4   Culturally responsive factors that promote effective communication and collaboration with individuals with exceptional learning needs, families, school personnel, and community members

CC10S3   Respectful and beneficial relationships between families and professionals

CC10S11   Observation, evaluation, and provision of feedback to paraeducators

No Time to Eat

Ms. King polished off the remains of her hamburger as she listened to Mrs. West outline the grade-level objectives for tomorrow's math lesson. Lunch planning meetings were typical for these two teachers. Ms. King, a fourth-grade teacher, had been co-teaching math with Mrs. West, the special education resource teacher, for the last two years. Their mutual respect for each other and their passion for seeing all students succeed led them to begin working closely together. Ms. King has a particularly challenging group of students this year, and Mrs. West has a full caseload of special education students. Of the 35 students in this class, 4 of them are identified for special education services.

The two teachers arranged their schedule to allow for Mrs. West to join this fourth-grade class for 50 minutes every day to co-deliver math instruction. They worked out a system for breaking up the responsibilities each day. Ms. King was the expert on how to pace the grade-level standards and Mrs. West planned for the differentiated instruction. Both took turns grading, preparing materials, and instructing. The process wasn't always easy, but it was rewarding, as all students in the class were making progress.

Their regular lunch meetings were getting harder and harder to manage. Both teachers had very busy schedules and these lunch meeting seemed to be the only time they could plan together. The more time they worked together, though, the longer it was taking to get through the planning. As their friendship grew, they found themselves slipping into conversations that had nothing to do with math. As Ms. King became more knowledgeable about modifying and adapting curriculum, they spent more time talking through each suggestion. Mrs. West developed strong opinions about the order in which content was presented and liked to suggest alternate materials. Although they weren't using a formalized planning tool, the teachers felt as though each lesson delivered was well planned and carefully executed.

Mrs. West and Ms. King have a great program in place, but the challenges in this collaborative relationship seem to be growing, not shrinking. Both teachers are becoming frustrated by the fact that they feel they never have time to eat!

QUESTIONS FOR REFLECTION

1. Identify the collaborative practices that seem to be working in this relationship. (CC10K1)
2. What collaborative planning strategies might these teachers use to help better utilize their time together? (CC10K2)

Homework

BY GLENNA STEWART

Jeff is a fourth-grade student diagnosed with autism. His parents had been strong advocates for their son since he was first diagnosed. It was important to the parents that Jeff continue to demonstrate academic growth and independence. Because they were strong advocates, an adversarial relationship had developed between the parents and the local school. Jeff's IEP meetings were attended by a multitude of people—the parents, advocates, attorneys, teachers, administrators, specialists, and others.

At the IEP meeting in October of Jeff's fourth-grade year, the teacher expressed concern about the fact that Jeff's homework was coming back incomplete or done incorrectly. The teacher wanted the parents to spend more time overseeing the homework and providing additional help to their son in correctly completing the homework.

The parents' position was that homework should be a reflection of what a child can do alone. If the child couldn't do it alone, then this was a sign that the school needed to provide additional instruction. This model had worked well with their other children and so they wanted to try the same thing with Jeff. They also said that there was limited time available for homework because Jeff was involved in numerous after-school activities. He had soccer, baseball, and other things that seemed to really be helping with his social skills. Since this was a big area of need for him, they felt their attention should be focused on this maybe even more than homework.

It was the position of the special educator and the general educator that the parents should sit down with Jeff to provide needed additional help or supervision to ensure that homework was complete and correct. They felt the responsibility for supervision and additional assistance fell to the parents. They also thought that maybe Jeff was involved in a few too many outside activities.

QUESTIONS FOR REFLECTION

1. How can Jeff's teacher plan and conduct collaborative conferences with the family, given the adversarial relationship they currently have? What can the school team do to move the relationship from an adversarial one to one that fosters a respectful and beneficial relationship? (CC10S5)
2. What should be the roles that the student, parent, and school take in ensuring Jeff's access to and completion of homework? (CC10K2)
3. What steps should the school team take to resolve their difference of opinion with the family and to respect the family's beliefs about homework? (CC10K4)

Get to Work!

BY AMY LARSEN

It's another day of managing paraeducators for Mrs. Chapman, the special education resource teacher at Noyes Elementary School. She works with a team of paraeducators at the school as they support a large number of students identified with special needs. School is about to begin and Mrs. Chapman is hoping that the paraeducators will carry out their responsibilities for the day just as they discussed together at their morning meeting.

Regular and daily duties are written out and posted for easy reference, and their morning meetings provide a time to check for questions in regard to daily duties. Mrs. Chapman elicits the paraeducators' input and considers their individual strengths and interests when delegating responsibilities. She even encourages them to decide between themselves who is going to do what and when.

Throughout the day, Mrs. Chapman has started to notice that the paraeducators socialize about personal stuff with each other at inappropriate times and often attend to their ringing cell phones. During these times, Mrs. Chapman notices that some students change their attention from their work to misbehaving. By the end of the day, many of the agreed-upon responsibilities are neglected or done poorly.

Although Mrs. Chapman continues to discuss her concerns with the paraeducators, this behavior continues. She really wants the adults to get along well, but believes that the paraeducators need to be a little more diligent in paying greater attention to the students. She fears confronting them too much, however, and is afraid they will react negatively to any criticism, thus jeopardizing student learning. Mrs. Chapman thought she had taken all the necessary steps to create a good working relationship with the paraeducators but now questions herself.

QUESTIONS FOR REFLECTION

1. What are some strategies Mrs. Chapman can implement to encourage the paraeducators to act more professionally? (CC10S11)
2. How can Mrs. Chapman make the role of the paraeducators more clear to them? (CC10K2)

Let the Teacher Teach

BY KIM MARTIN

Noel has returned to school after being held out for a year. Her parents were very unhappy with Noel's last school and so decided she should just stay home. They've now decided to have her return to school. Mr. Simon, the special education teacher, is frustrated because Noel seems to resist all forms of instruction he's tried and Noel frequently runs away when they are outside the classroom. Noel's parents have also requested that Noel receive her related services—physical therapy, occupational therapy, and speech therapy—during the morning, since Noel is most alert during those hours. Mr. Simon also knows the morning hours are important in Noel's second-grade class and is worried about her missing class activities for her therapies. This has made scheduling a difficult challenge for Mr. Simon. Now the family is requesting that Noel participate in a specialized structured discrete trial instructional program, which will mean she will be pulled out of her second-grade classroom even more. Mr. Simon wants to work collaboratively with the family but has found the multiple competing demands to be difficult.

QUESTIONS FOR REFLECTION

1. What could Mr. Simon do to try to improve the collaborative nature of his relationship with Noel's parents? (CC10K3, CC10S3)
2. How can Mr. Simon reconcile the multiple competing demands he feels he faces when developing an appropriate educational program for Noel? (CC10S6)

The Ties that Bind...

From his first day in school, Henry was seemingly eager to work. During his first year working with Mrs. May, the special education support teacher, Henry had learned his letters and sounds, learned math concepts, and displayed a responsible attitude toward his schoolwork and in his interactions with his peers. Over the next three years working with Mrs. May, Henry continued to show tremendous growth. At the end of his third-grade year, Henry appeared adjusted to school and ready to transition to the upper-elementary group supported by Mrs. Moore. Mrs. May and Mrs. Moore met to plan the transition and appeared to be "on the same page" in regard to Henry's needs. They decided to transition him into Mrs. Moore's group during summer school.

Over the summer, Henry displayed some troubling behaviors. He acted aggressively toward other students and defaced school property. Mrs. May and Mrs. Moore had repeated meetings to discuss the situation and Mrs. May even met with Henry to help figure out what to do. Henry promised Mrs. May that he would behave better but all of their discussions didn't seem to be helping. Both teachers thought it might just be a reaction to the transition that would fade away as the school year commenced.

When September came, Henry did in fact come to school and behave appropriately. In October, however, he started to misbehave again. He acted aggressively and was defiant about not doing his work. He even threatened to hurt Mrs. Moore. Many times, Henry would run out of his classroom looking for Mrs. May. Mrs. Moore and Mrs. May met again to discuss the situation, with Mrs. Moore most interested in hearing from Mrs. May about possible triggers for Henry's problematic behavior. Mrs. May said she had never seen these behaviors so couldn't provide much information. The teachers discussed possible ways to respond to Henry's behavior and seemed to have a good set of ideas to use in addressing the situation.

As the weeks went by, the behavior problems continued. The situation deteriorated and Mrs. May became very concerned about Henry, as was the principal. She offered to help Mrs. Moore but was told that Henry was no longer her responsibility. With Henry's behavior at its worst, the relationship between Mrs. May and Mrs. Moore was strained. When Mrs. May ran into Henry on the playground, she would talk with him but it was clear that Mrs. Moore did not appreciate her efforts to help. By January, Mrs. May learned that Henry was being transferred to another school. Mrs. May was very upset because she felt that there must have been something she could have done to help in this situation.

QUESTIONS FOR REFLECTION

1. What suggestions can you make for working with teachers who seem "territorial" about their students? (CC10S6)
2. What could have been done to ease Henry's transition? Could Mrs. May have better communicated with other school personnel about Henry's needs? (CC10S9)

What More Can I Do?

BY JOY DYE

Kayleigh is a kindergarten student who is big for her age and who has to sit on a chair during rug time because she cannot sit with her legs folded or outstretched on the floor. It is just too uncomfortable for her to manage that kind of body position on the floor. Mr. Strode, Kayleigh's teacher, had observed in the first few weeks of school that Kayleigh also has difficulty walking. She often trips over her feet and falls. Once she is down on the floor, it is very hard and laborious for her to get back up. He also noted that her fine motor skills were very poor. She could not cut using scissors and she was unable to form a strong pencil grip when writing or coloring.

Upon reviewing Kayleigh's records, Mr. Strode found that she qualified for special education services with the label of "developmental delay," and he also discovered that Kayleigh and her family receive support from a social worker. She lives at home with her mom, dad, and baby brother.

Mr. Strode asked the adaptive physical education teacher assigned to his school to come and observe Kayleigh during recess to see how they could design activities to help support Kayleigh in the motoric area. However, since Kayleigh's parents would keep her home from school quite often—at least one day a week—the APE specialist had difficulty completing the observation. After about a month, she finally completed the observation and provided suggestions to help Kayleigh develop both fine and gross motor skills.

When it was time to arrange the IEP meeting, Mr. Strode tried calling Kayleigh's parents to set up the meeting. He wanted to discuss three areas of concern he had regarding Kayleigh: (1) her fine/gross motor abilities, (2) her frequent absences, and (3) her frequent incomplete homework (she hardly ever turned in completed homework). He also called the social worker who was listed in her records. After leaving three phone messages with no response from Kayleigh's parents, Mr. Strode finally typed a letter and had it sent home with Kayleigh. Also, after numerous attempts to reach Kayleigh's social worker, Mr. Strode was finally able to connect with her. He explained that he would like to set up an IEP meeting with Kayleigh's parents to discuss his concerns with her parents and to come up with a plan that would best meet Kayleigh's needs and he would like the social worker to attend the meeting.

Finally, after two weeks of trying, Mr. Strode was able to set a date that both Kayleigh's parents and social worker would be able to make. Mr. Strode also invited the APE specialist and the principal. The week of the IEP meeting, Mr. Strode sent a letter home reminding Kayleigh's parents. Finally, the day and time came to meet with Kayleigh's parents. However, Kayleigh's parents did not show up, nor did Kayleigh's social worker. The social worker called later and explained that she had to go out of town on an emergency.

Mr. Strode was upset. He spent so much energy and time arranging an IEP meeting and the parents did not even show up. What could Mr. Strode, the APE specialist, and the principal do?

QUESTIONS FOR REFLECTION

1. How can Mr. Strode get Kayleigh's parents involved in her IEP and develop a more active relationship with the school? Should he expect the parents to be active participants at school? Why or why not? (CC10K1, CC10S3)

2. What support should Mr. Strode expect from the social worker? What role should the APE teacher take? (CC10S2)

Mrs. Who?

Dr. Janks was interested in visiting Mrs. Jones's preschool classroom. He was visiting her because he was charged with assessing her performance in terms of how well she was implementing instruction that fit the state standards. He had been impressed with Mrs. Jones in their earlier discussions and was intrigued by how she described her inclusive preschool program. When he arrived at the school site, Dr. Janks followed the instructions that said all visitors should go to the school office first. He was then surprised when the office staff didn't recognize Mrs. Jones's name nor did they know where her class was located. He thought perhaps he had arrived at the wrong school so checked his records and showed the staff. They said that the address and phone number were for this school but they didn't know Mrs. Jones. One of the staff members said she would go see if anyone in the teachers' lounge knew Mrs. Jones. She returned a few minutes later and said that she knew how to find Mrs. Jones. Mrs. Jones was the "helper" in the preschool program on site and Dr. Janks was directed there. Dr. Janks left the office wondering how inclusive the program would be if the office staff didn't even know the teacher's name!

QUESTIONS FOR REFLECTION

1. Was Dr. Janks correct to be surprised at the school staff's response? Did this really reflect the status of the teacher at the school? What steps could be taken to increase the collaborative nature of the preschool program? (CC10S6)
2. What do you hypothesize are the roles that Mrs. Jones fulfills in the preschool program if she is viewed as a "helper"? (CC10K2)

Can I Change Mrs. Asper?

BY JOY DYE

Mrs. Hill was excited to start the new school year. She had just transferred to a new school and was looking forward to the change. She prepared her new classroom for her kindergarten and first-graders, and had her lessons for the first week ready. The day before school started, Mrs. Asper, the paraeducator, came in and introduced herself to Mrs. Hill. She explained that she had been working with this class and at this school for the past 20 years. She went on to tell Mrs. Hill that the past 6 years had been filled with temporary teachers, and that she just loves working with the little kids. This first meeting went well. Mrs. Hill thought that it would be nice to work with someone who has many years of experience in working with children with disabilities.

After the first month of working with Mrs. Asper in the classroom, Mrs. Hill realized that she had a problem that she was going to have to solve. Mrs. Asper raised her voice when working with the students in her group. Instead of offering positive feedback and reinforcements, she focused on the negative behavior and used discipline to try to correct the behavior. This caused the students to become frustrated and not willing to go to Mrs. Asper's group to learn. Also, Mrs. Hill noticed that Mrs. Asper either was not able to or chose not to follow the simple lesson plans she left with Mrs. Asper to use when the students came to her group. Often she would just "do her own thing."

Mrs. Hill sat down with Mrs. Asper while the some of the students were at the computer lab and others in the library. She discussed her concerns, and Mrs. Asper seemed to understand and she agreed to spend some time observing Mrs. Hill teaching a lesson and modeling the positive reward system. This helped for the next few weeks, but eventually the yelling returned and the lessons were not being done as explained.

Another problem that affected the whole class was that Mrs. Asper called in sick about two times a week. Mrs. Hill asked Mrs. Asper to please request a specific substitute when she was going to be out. However, Mrs. Asper never followed through with this request, which disrupted the entire class because too many different people were coming in and out of the classroom.

Mrs. Hill had already met with Mrs. Asper once. It seemed to help for a little while, but now things seem to be getting worse.

QUESTIONS FOR REFLECTION

1. What strategies would you suggest Mrs. Hill use to help Mrs. Asper follow through with her classroom procedures? (CC10S11)
2. How can Mrs. Hill use group problem-solving skills to resolve this situation? (CC10S7)

CEC Knowledge and Skill Base for All Beginning Special Education Teachers: Common Core Standards

Special Education Standard #1: Foundations

Knowledge:

CC1K1	Models, theories, and philosophies that form the basis for special education practice
CC1K2	Laws, policies, and ethical principles regarding behavior management planning and implementation
CC1K3	Relationship of special education to the organization and function of educational agencies
CC1K4	Rights and responsibilities of students, parents, teachers, and other professionals, and schools related to exceptional learning needs
CC1K5	Issues in definition and identification of individuals with exceptional learning needs, including those from culturally and linguistically diverse backgrounds
CC1K6	Issues, assurances, and due process rights related to assessment, eligibility, and placement within a continuum of services
CC1K7	Family systems and the role of families in the educational process
CC1K8	Historical points of view and contribution of culturally diverse groups
CC1K9	Impact of the dominant culture on shaping schools and the individuals who study and work in them
CC1K10	Potential impact of differences in values, languages, and customs that can exist between the home and school

Skill:

CC1S1	Articulation of personal philosophy of special education

CEC
Knowledge
and Skill Base
for All
Beginning
Special
Education
Teachers:
Common Core
Standards

Special Education Standard #2:
Development and Characteristics of Learners

Knowledge:

CC2K1	Typical and atypical human growth and development
CC2K2	Educational implications of characteristics of various exceptionalities
CC2K3	Characteristics and effects of the cultural and environmental milieu of the individual with exceptional learning needs and the family
CC2K4	Family systems and the role of families in supporting development
CC2K5	Similarities and differences of individuals with and without exceptional learning needs
CC2K6	Similarities and differences among individuals with exceptional learning needs
CC2K7	Effects of various medications on individuals with exceptional learning needs

Special Education Standard #3:
Individual Learning Differences

Knowledge:

CC3K1	Effects an exceptional condition(s) can have on an individual's life
CC3K2	Impact of learners' academic and social abilities, attitudes, interests, and values on instruction and career development
CC3K3	Variations in beliefs, traditions, and values across and within cultures and their effects on relationships among individuals with exceptional learning needs, family, and schooling
CC3K4	Cultural perspectives influencing the relationships among families, schools, and communities as related to instruction
CC3K5	Differing ways of learning of individuals with exceptional learning needs, including those from culturally diverse backgrounds, and strategies for addressing these differences

Special Education Standard #4:
Instructional Strategies

Skills:

CC4S1	Strategies to facilitate integration into various settings
CC4S2	Individuals taught to use self-assessment, problem solving, and other cognitive strategies to meet their needs
CC4S3	Selection, adaptation, and use of instructional strategies and materials according to characteristics of the individual with exceptional learning needs
CC4S4	Strategies to facilitate maintenance and generalization of skills across learning environments
CC4S5	Procedures to increase the individual's self-awareness, self-management, self-control, self-reliance, and self-esteem
CC4S6	Strategies that promote successful transitions for individuals with exceptional learning needs

Special Education Standard #5:
Learning Environments and Social Interactions

*CEC
Knowledge
and Skill Base
for All
Beginning
Special
Education
Teachers:
Common Core
Standards*

Knowledge:

CC5K1	Demands of learning environments
CC5K2	Basic classroom management theories and strategies for individuals with exceptional learning needs
CC5K3	Effective management of teaching and learning
CC5K4	Teacher attitudes and behaviors that influence behavior of individuals with exceptional learning needs
CC5K5	Social skills needed for educational and other environments
CC5K6	Strategies for crisis prevention and intervention
CC5K7	Strategies for preparing individuals to live harmoniously and productively in a culturally diverse world
CC5K8	Ways to create learning environments that allow individuals to retain and appreciate their own and each others' respective language and cultural heritage
CC5K9	Ways specific cultures are negatively stereotyped
CC5K10	Strategies used by diverse populations to cope with a legacy of former and continuing racism

Skills:

CC5S1	Creation of safe, equitable, positive, and supportive learning environment in which diversities are valued
CC5S2	Identification of realistic expectations for personal and social behavior in various settings
CC5S3	Identification of supports needed for integration into various program placements
CC5S4	Learning environments that encourage active participation in individual and group activities
CC5S5	Learning environment modified to manage behaviors
CC5S6	Use of performance data and information from all stakeholders to make or suggest modifications in learning environments
CC5S7	Establishment and maintenance of rapport with individuals with and without exceptional learning needs
CC5S8	Self-advocacy taught
CC5S9	Creation of an environment that encourages self-advocacy and increased independence
CC5S10	Use of effective and varied behavior management strategies
CC5S11	Use of the least intensive behavior management strategy consistent with the needs of the individual with exceptional learning needs
CC5S12	Design and management of daily routines
CC5S13	Organization, development, and maintenance of learning environments that support positive intracultural and intercultural experiences.
CC5S14	Mediation of controversial intercultural issues among students within the learning environment in ways that enhance any culture, group, or person
CC5S15	Structure, direct, and support the activities of paraeducators, volunteers, and tutors
CC5S16	Use of universal precautions

116
APPENDIX A

*CEC
Knowledge
and Skill Base
for All
Beginning
Special
Education
Teachers:
Common Core
Standards*

Special Education Standard #6: Language

Knowledge:

CC6K1	Effects of cultural and linguistic differences on growth and development
CC6K2	Characteristics of one's own culture and use of language and the ways in which these can differ from other cultures and uses of languages
CC6K3	Ways of behaving and communicating among cultures that can lead to misinterpretation and misunderstanding
CC6K4	Augmentative and assistive communication strategies

Skills:

CC6S1	Strategies to support and enhance communication skills of individuals with exceptional learning needs
CC6S2	Communication strategies and resources to facilitate understanding of subject matter for students whose primary language is not the dominant language

Special Education Standard #7: Instructional Planning

Knowledge:

CC7K1	Theories and research that form the basis of curriculum development and instructional practice
CC7K2	Scope and sequences of general and special curricula
CC7K3	National, state or provincial, and local curricula standards
CC7K4	Technology for planning and managing the teaching and learning environment
CC7K5	Roles and responsibilities of the paraeducator related to instruction, intervention, and direct service

Skills:

CC7S1	Identification and prioritization of areas of the general curriculum and accommodations for individuals with exceptional learning needs
CC7S2	Development and implementation of comprehensive, longitudinal individualized programs in collaboration with team members
CC7S3	Involvement of the individual and family in setting instructional goals and monitoring progress
CC7S4	Use of functional assessments to develop intervention plans
CC7S5	Use of task analysis
CC7S6	Sequence, implementation, and evaluation of individualized learning objectives
CC7S7	Affective, social, and life skills integrated with academic curricula
CC7S8	Development and selection of instructional content, resources, and strategies that respond to cultural, linguistic, and gender differences
CC7S9	Incorporation and implemention of instructional and assistive technology into the educational program
CC7S10	Preparation of lesson plans
CC7S11	Preparation and organization of materials to implement daily lesson plans
CC7S12	Use of instructional time effectively
CC7S13	Responsive adjustments to instruction based on continual observations
CC7S14	Preparation of individuals to exhibit self-enhancing behavior in response to societal attitudes and actions

Special Education Standard #8: Assessment

117

APPENDIX A

*CEC
Knowledge
and Skill Base
for All
Beginning
Special
Education
Teachers:
Common Core
Standards*

Knowledge:

CC8K1	Basic terminology used in assessment
CC8K2	Legal provisions and ethical principles regarding assessment of individuals
CC8K3	Screening, prereferral, referral, and classification procedures
CC8K4	Use and limitations of assessment instruments
CC8K5	National, state or provincial, and local accommodations and modifications

Skills:

CC8S1	Gathering of relevant background information
CC8S2	Administration of nonbiased formal and informal assessments
CC8S3	Use of technology to conduct assessments
CC8S4	Development or modification of individualized assessment strategies
CC8S5	Interpretation of information from formal and informal assessments
CC8S6	Use of assessment information in making eligibility, program, and placement decisions for individuals with exceptional learning needs, including those from culturally and/or linguistically diverse backgrounds
CC8S7	Assessment results reported to all stakeholders using effective communication skills
CC8S8	Evaluation of instruction and monitoring of progress of individuals with exceptional learning needs
CC8S9	Development or modification of individualized assessment strategies
CC8S10	Creation and maintenance of records

Special Education Standard #9: Professional and Ethical Practices

Knowledge:

CC9K1	Personal cultural biases and differences that affect one's teaching
CC9K2	Importance of the teacher serving as a model for individuals with exceptional learning needs
CC9K3	Continuum of lifelong professional development
CC9K4	Methods to remain current regarding research-validated practice

Skills:

CC9S1	Practice within the CEC Code of Ethics and other standards of the profession
CC9S2	High standards of competence and integrity and sound judgment in the practice of the professional
CC9S3	Ethical action when advocating for appropriate services
CC9S4	Professional activities in compliance with applicable laws and policies
CC9S5	Demonstration of commitment to developing the highest education and quality-of-life potential of individuals with exceptional learning needs
CC9S6	Demonstration of sensitivity for the culture, language, religion, gender, disability, socioeconomic status, and sexual orientation of individuals
CC9S7	Practice within one's skill limit and obtaining assistance as needed
CC9S8	Use of verbal, nonverbal, and written language effectively
CC9S9	Self-evaluation of instruction

118
....

APPENDIX A

CEC
Knowledge
and Skill Base
for All
Beginning
Special
Education
Teachers:
Common Core
Standards

CC9S10	Information access on exceptionalities
CC9S11	Reflection on one's practice to improve instruction and guide professional growth
CC9S12	Professional activities that benefit individuals with exceptional learning needs, their families, and one's colleagues

Special Education Standard #10: Collaboration

Knowledge:

CC10K1	Models and strategies of consultation and collaboration
CC10K2	Roles of individuals with exceptional learning needs, families, and school and community personnel in the planning of an individualized program
CC10K3	Concerns of families of individuals with exceptional learning needs and strategies to help address these concerns
CC10K4	Culturally responsive factors that promote effective communication and collaboration with individuals with exceptional learning needs, families, school personnel, and community members

Skills:

CC10S1	Confidential communication about individuals with exceptional learning needs
CC10S2	Collaboration with families and others in assessment of individuals with exceptional learning needs
CC10S3	Respectful and beneficial relationships between families and professionals
CC10S4	Assistance for individuals with exceptional learning needs and their families in becoming active participants in the educational team
CC10S5	Collaborative conferences with individuals with exceptional learning needs and their families
CC10S6	Collaboration with school personnel and community members in integrating individuals with exceptional learning needs into various settings
CC10S7	Use of group problem-solving skills to develop, implement, and evaluate collaborative activities
CC10S8	Model techniques and coach others in the use of instructional methods and accommodations.
CC10S9	Communication with school personnel about the characteristics and needs of individuals with exceptional learning needs
CC10S10	Communication with families of individuals with exceptional learning needs from diverse backgrounds.
CC10S11	Observation, evaluation, and provision of feedback to paraeducators

Vignette Cross-References

	Foundations	Development	Individual Differences	Instructional Strategies
Chapter 2: Foundations				
What Do I Believe?	Personal philosophy		Similarities and differences	
The Silent Parents	Culture/Family			
Too Many Boys	Culture/Classification		Cultural differences	
Differing Beliefs	Educational systems			
When Federal Mandates Attack	Educational systems			
To Evaluate or Not?	Identification/Culture	Typical/Atypical development		
Ready or Not . . .	Educational systems/ Culture			Facilitate integration
Resource or Self-Contained Class	Family/Culture			
Retention and Social Promotion	Systems/Culture			
Baby Steps	History culture			
Chapter 3: Development and Characteristics of Learners				
Surgery Will Make It All Better	Home/School	Typical/Atypical development		
The "Monster" in My Classroom		Similarities/ Differences	Differing ways of learning	
What a Label Changes		Implications of labels		
Elmo		Typical/Atypical development/ Culture		
Should He Graduate?		Implications of labels		
Are They Ready?		Similarities/ Differences		
He's Not Autistic, Is He?		Similarities/ Differences		
Is Medication the Right Thing?		Medication		

Learning Environments	Language	Instructional Planning	Assessment	Professional Practices	Collaboration
				Reflect on practice	
		Involve families			Family participation
			Eligibility		
				Laws and policies	Parents
		Curricula standards			
			Referral		
Positive environments					
Supports	Facilitate understanding				
Performance data				Ethics	
Integration					Family/Culture
				Sensitivity	Families
				Ethics	
			Classification		Team roles
Peers	Communicate with families			Communicate with families	
Integration		Prioritize			
			Placement		
			Monitor progress	Access information	
				Ethics	Community personnel

	Foundations	Development	Individual Differences	Instructional Strategies
Chapter 4: Individual Learning Differences				
She Can't Read?			Academic abilities	
Please Try before Referring			Academic abilities	Teacher attitudes and beliefs
Don't Judge a Book by Its Cover			Variations in beliefs	
Don't Jump to Conclusions	Dominant culture		Cultural perspectives	
I Hate My 504 Plan!	Laws		Effects of exceptionality	
Placement Tug-of-War			Cultural perspectives	
Who's to Blame?	Educational systems		Impact of abilities	
What Do We Do Now?	Educational systems		Impact of abilities	
Another Episode			Effects of exceptionality	
Chapter 5: Instructional Strategies				
Packaged Programs Are Not "Special"				Adapt instruction
Josh's Wasting Time				Transitions
Who Is Right?	Educational system			Facilitate integration
Gilbert "Sounds" It Out		Similarities/ Differences		Self-awareness
Forgetting to Count				Generalization/ Transitions
Teaching to Read	Rights and responsibilities			Adapt strategies
How Far Can She Stretch?			Differing ways of learning	Adapt strategies
Finding the Right "Fit"			Differing ways of learning	Adapt strategies
It Works?				Adapt strategies
What Was She Thinking?	Educational systems			Adapt materials

Learning Environments	Language	Instructional Planning	Assessment	Professional Practices	Collaboration
				High standards/ Ethics	Team roles
	Misunderstanding				Concerns of families
				Cultural biases	
		Responsive adjustments			
				Cultural biases	Communicate with families
					Team roles
Encourage active participation				Ethics	
Crisis prevention					Team roles
	Curricula standards			Laws/Ethics	
Positive environments		Self-enhancing behaviors			
				Advocacy	
Supports					
		Responsive adjustments		Self-evaluation	
				High standards	
				Self-evaluation	
					Team roles
		Scope and sequence		Laws and policies	
					Team roles

123

	Foundations	Development	Individual Differences	Instructional Strategies
Chapter 6: Learning Environments and Social Interactions				
Did Katie Receive a Fair Chance?	Due process			
What's an Aide to Do?				Facilitate integration
How Does Ned Fit In?				Facilitate integration
How Far Can an Aide Go?				
Study Skills or Homework?				Self-management
Going around in Circles				
Michael Deserves a Chance	Laws/Due process			
Stop Teasing Me	Dominant culture			
Chapter 7: Language				
Can I Do It?				Adapt instruction
Whose Language Barrier?	Home and school			
Bridging Language Barriers				
What Have I Gotten Myself Into?		Cultural perspectives		
Labeling Dilemma				
"Toilet, Water Closet, Bano . . ."				
Twin Talk			Typical/Atypical development	
Who Speaks for Joey?				Self-awareness
Lost in Translation				Adapt instruction

124

Learning Environments	Language	Instructional Planning	Assessment	Professional Practices	Collaboration
Teacher attitudes/ Use of data				Advocacy	
Behavior management					Support paraeducators
Manage behaviors					Integration
Manage behaviors		Roles of paraeducators			Collaborate with families
Manage routines					Collaborate with general education teachers
Behavior management		Functional assessment			Collaborate with community
Crisis prevention				CEC code of ethics	
Positive intercultural experiences					Cultural responsive
	Facilitate understanding of subject matter	Prioritize			
	Use of language				Communicate with families
	Enhance communication skills		Resport results		Communicate with families
	Facilitate understanding of subject matter			Reflect on practice	
	Effects of linguistic differences			Eligibility/ Placement	Laws
	Augmentative communication		Background information	Personal biases	
Social skills	Effects of linguistic differences				
Active participation	Misinterpretation				
	Misunderstanding				Communicate with families

	Foundations	Development	Individual Differences	Instructional Strategies
Chapter 8: Instructional Planning				
No Supplies for Mr. Kennedy	Educational systems			
This Could Work				Facilitate integration
Planning for Mark		Differing ways of learning		
I Did It!				
How Will I Do It?				
Is This Okay?				Facilitate integration
How Many Grade Levels?	Educational systems			
Teaching Addition			Similarities and differences	
Chapter 9: Assessment				
How to Test?			Similarities and differences	
Are You Sure?			Similarities and differences	
Finding a Way		Typical/Atypical development		
Going through the Motions	Due process			
Meaningful Monitoring				
How Much Can I Do?			Differing ways of learning	
Too Much Already!				
Am I Cheating?	Educational systems			

Learning Environments	Language	Instructional Planning	Assessment	Professional Practices	Collaboration
		Scope and sequence		Advocacy	
		Individualized programs			Models of collaboration
		Individualized programs		High standards	
Manage daily routines		Lesson planning	Program decisions		
Manage daily routines		Individualized programs		Ethics	Collaborate with school personnel
		Positive learning environment			Collaborate with school personnel
Manage daily routines		Scope and sequence			
	Linguistic differences	Responsive adjustments			
			Limitations of tests	Self-evaluation	
			Modify assessments		Collaborate with school personnel
			Monitor progress		
	Augmentative communication		Program decisions	High standards/ Advocacy	
		Scope and sequence	Report assessments		Communicate with families
Manage daily routines			Legal principles		
Manage daily routines			Monitor progress		Collaborate with community
		Curricula standards	Accommodations/ Modifications		

	Foundations	Development	Individual Differences	Instructional Strategies
Chapter 10: Professionalism and Ethical Practices				
What Do I Ask For?	Educational systems			Facilitate integration
Where Is She?				
Why Isn't Your Homework Done?	Family systems			
Setting Limits?	Impact of culture			
The Loss of a Talented Teacher	Educational systems			
A New System			Differing ways of learning	
Should I Ask for Help?				
Paperwork Overload				
Why Are You Teaching?	Rights and responsibilities			
Chapter 11: Collaboration				
No Time to Eat			Differing ways of learning	
Homework	Family systems			Adapt strategies
Get to Work!				
Let the Teacher Teach				
The Ties that Bind . . .				
What More Can I Do?	Family systems			
Mrs. Who?	Educational systems			Facilitate integration
Can I Change Mrs. Asper?				

Learning Environments	Language	Instructional Planning	Assessment	Professional Practices	Collaboration
				Obtain assistance	
		Individualize		Highest educational potential	Team roles
				Professional practices	Concerns of families
Intercultural issues				Advocacy	
		Curricula standards		Integrity	
	Augmentative communication			Access information	
Behavior management				Obtain assistance	Team roles
			Maintain records	High standards	Communicate with families
		Use instructional time effectively		High standards	
		Time management			Collaborate with school personnel
					Collaborative conferences
Classroom management		Time management			Observe/Evaluate paraeducators
Effective management		Individualize programs			Family concerns
Behavior management				High standards	Collaborate with school personnel
				Advocacy	Collaborate with community
					Integration
Classroom management		Lesson planning			Problem-solving skills

Appendix C

Annotated Vignette Summaries

Foundations

What Do I Believe?

Hansford finds it challenging to articulate his personal philosophy of education. What exactly does he believe? Even more challenging, Hansford wonders how he will be able to actually implement this philosophy into practice.

The Silent Parents

Ms. Wash wonders how to increase the "silent parents'" participation in the IEP process. She considers the challenges that language barriers and socioeconomic status bring to this relationship. Ms. Wash desires a more personal connection with her parents but isn't sure how to go about this.

Too Many Boys

How is it that Mr. Kim has so many boys on his caseload? He isn't convinced that all these boys identified as learning disabled actually require special education services. Mr. Kim questions classroom practices that might be causing boys at this school site to look more delayed than they actually are.

Differing Beliefs

At Ms. Petrie's school, a task force is formed to address a court order for her large district to move students out of segregated special education settings and into the least restrictive environment. Ms. Petrie is honored to be asked to serve as chair of the committee but is then surprised by the parents' comments about wanting to keep their children in the protective special education setting rather than a less restrictive setting. The staff wonders how they will be able to convince the parents that their children will be safe when education in the least restrictive environment.

When Federal Mandates Attack

Graduate students, working as special education teachers, share their concerns about district interpretation of federal mandates. Teachers are being asked to implement curriculum and IEP objectives that do not compliment best practices. These teachers are struggling with making the intent of the law and the actual practices coincide.

To Evaluate or Not?

Lolo was driving the staff at Ridgemont Elementary School crazy. He hadn't yet mastered a dominant use of one language and he displayed aggressive behaviors. The school team was waiting to assess him, but there were many outside factors that needed to be addressed first. How could the school meet his needs in the mean time?

Ready or Not. . .

Brian's parents want him included in general education classes as soon as possible. Brian is hesitant, as he had a negative experience in general education before. His parents don't want to wait any longer but his teacher isn't sure he is "ready."

Resource or Self-Contained Class

Josephine doesn't like school, or so she told her teacher. She doesn't perform well on tests and isn't making progress. Although she struggles with academics, Josephine continually shows her creativity in dance, art, and stories. Her teacher struggles with the decision to keep her in general education when she continues to do so poorly in academics.

Retention and Social Promotion

The IEP team has suggested that Henry Tatupu be retained but his special education teacher feels that retaining him is not in alignment with the mandates of IDEIA.

Baby Steps

Mrs. Hall describes three years of teaching Leslie and developing relationships with Leslie and her mother. This case provides examples of challenges in providing appropriate supports and providing education in the least restrictive environment.

Development and Characteristics of Learners

Surgery Will Make It All Better

Quentin's teacher enjoys working with him and is pleased that he is succeeding in his middle school math, science, and computer classes. At the IEP meeting, the teacher informs the family that Quentin is making progress in all his classes and the family then asks if the teacher if she thinks surgery for his CP will now make him normal. The teacher isn't sure how to best help the family understand Quentin's developmental status.

The "Monster" in My Classroom

After reading Mandy's records, Ms. Dumas was really worried about this student who sounded so challenging on paper. The next morning, she ran into the general education teacher who would have Mandy in her class and she shared her concerns about Mandy. When Mandy came to school a little later, they were both surprised to meet this somewhat shy and polite student who struggled academically but was not the "monster" she seemed to be on paper.

What a Label Changes

Ms. Montel really loves working with James, so she is worried now that James has been labeled as having "autistic-like" tendencies. Her general education classroom is now inundated with specialists working with him. She thinks it was somehow easier to work with James when he was just considered a difficult student, but one with whom she enjoyed working. This vignette provides an opportunity to discuss the impact of labeling someone as "not normal."

Elmo

Mrs. Marley was pleased when a parent suggested having a classroom birthday party for her son. Mrs. Marley knew that her middle school aged students really liked having special events like parties. She was therefore shocked when this parent came to school with an Elmo character. She knew how the middle schoolers would respond and wondered how she could turn this situation into something positive.

Should He Graduate?

Ara's family was confused by all the terms that were used at his last IEP meeting. They assumed Ara would graduate from high school with a diploma but then the staff started to talk about things like a "certificate of completion" and "exit exams." They were confused.

Are They Ready?

Mr. Kim was pleased that his pre-K students were progressing. He wondered, however, if the almost 5-year-olds were really ready to make the transition to kindergarten. How could he ensure their readiness?

He's Not Autistic, Is He?

Daniel was given the label of autism in preschool. In first grade, he did not like changes in his schedules but did not tantrum as he did in preschool. He also made progress, although he was a little behind the majority of kids. As his annual IEP meeting approaches, the team struggles with whether to change Daniel's label or exit him from special education. Will problems arise later?

Is Medication the Right Thing?

Mr. Solis struggles with the issue of students on medication. Although he is seeing positive changes in Hyun after he started using medication, Mr. Solis wonders if this is the best choice for his students.

Individual Learning Differences

She Can't Read?

Carrie's parents couldn't believe what they were hearing. Carrie's special education teacher just told them that she had not been teaching Carrie to read, as was included in her IEP, because the teacher said, "Kids like Carrie can't learn to read." Carrie's parents decided to ensure she was taught to read.

Please Try before Referring

Mrs. Nguyen knew that her school was committed to seeing that it appropriately identified kids with disabilities. She also knew, however, that teachers often didn't really make a commitment to provide support before they referred a child to special education. They often felt stretched too far.

Don't Judge a Book by Its Cover

When the parents of one student with mild disabilities came to school on the first day, Mr. Lance was surprised to hear the parents say that their child must have been assigned to the wrong class, as their child was not "retarded" and all the other children in the class must be because they were in wheelchairs. How will Mr. Lance help the parents understand the individual differences of his students and the parents' misunderstanding of what it means to use a wheelchair?

Don't Jump to Conclusions

Mrs. E. could not believe the mistake she had made in pushing Huong's family to have him participate in household tasks. She thought they had resisted because they were being overly protective of him due to his disabilities, and so she had engaged in many efforts to change their thinking about his abilities. After all this effort, Huong's sister finally asked Mrs. E. why she was pushing so much on these domestic tasks, because in Huong's family, women performed those tasks. This vignette provides an opportunity to discuss jumping to conclusions based on assumptions about cultural beliefs.

I Hate My 504 Plan!

After years of struggling in school, Billy was tested for special education but it wasn't clear that he was eligible. Billy did not want to be labeled as a special education resource program student anyway. A Section 504 Plan was therefore developed, but appeared to mean little in high school, as the plan was not followed. The parents tried to enforce the 504 Plan but Billy finally said he had had enough of the 504 Plan.

Placement Tug-of-War

Lola was placed in a general education class and performed well. When the team considered resource support for Lola, her mother requested placement in a self-contained class where an adult would always be with her child. The team went along, but Lola quickly appeared bored in the self-contained class. The teacher kept increasing the curriculum demands but really felt that Lola needed to return to the general education class.

Who's to Blame?

Sean recently moved to a new district. Sean's teacher, Ms. Smith, is surprised by how delayed he is and how this isn't noted in his records. Nor are there records that Sean received early intervention after he was born prematurely, weighing in at 1.5 pounds. How will Ms. Smith help Sean and help his parents understand how delayed he is? Why didn't someone intervene earlier?

What Do We Do Now?

Jibril had initially been found eligible for special education services because of learning disabilities. As his muscular dystrophy progressed, his physical needs seem to be outweighing his academic needs and the school isn't sure how to accommodate for his physical needs.

Another Episode

John is once again sorry after a destructive episode but this doesn't help his teacher in figuring out how best to stop these destructive episodes from happening again.

Instructional Strategies

Packaged Programs Are Not "Special"

Mr. Hall is frustrated by the endless assortment of packaged curricula that his district adopts each school year. These programs often go against everything he has learned about individualizing instruction and he doesn't know how to explain to the parents of his students that they haven't made progress on their IEP objectives because he has to spend so much time on these mandated programs.

Josh's Wasting Time

Josh feels that high school is just a waste of time and so can hardly wait to go to his job each day. He wants to do something that makes sense to him, which provides food for thought about how his school could provide instruction that "makes sense to him."

Who Is Right?

A program for students with the label of autism serves these students for kindergarten and first grade at a local elementary school. After first grade, the students are expected to return to their neighborhood school. Most parents don't

136
....

APPENDIX C

Annotated
Vignette
Summaries

agree with this move and so resort to due process. The teacher in the program isn't sure how best to address the concerns of these parents, the district policy, and the frustration of the principal over all the time spent on due process.

Gilbert "Sounds" It Out

Gilbert is in third grade and he is struggling with his new phonics instruction program. Ms. Valentine worries about him and so is very excited on the day that he finally is able to distinguish between *tale* and *tell* by noticing that "they almost sound the same but they look different when someone says them."

Forgetting to Count

Ira can successfully complete basic counting and arithmetic problems when in Mr. Westfall's classroom, but when he returns to his homeroom, he seems to forget how to count. His teachers are concerned about how to help Ira transfer the knowledge he shows in one environment to another.

Teaching to Read

Mr. Page is surprised to find that one of his high school students does not read beyond a first-grade level. When the student asks for help learning to read, Mr. Page is excited but also nervous and uncertain about how best to help a high schooler learn to read.

How Far Can She Stretch?

Mrs. Stone has a new student with autism, Alex, in her class and is trying to figure out how best to accommodate his needs along with all her other students. She appreciates Alex's one-on-one aide but feels that she is being stretched too far in trying to meet Alex's needs as well as accomplish all the other things she must.

Finding the Right "Fit"

Mr. Han asks why Samuel isn't just placed in "one of those really special classes." He doesn't feel that the instructional modifications required for Samuel to succeed in his second-grade class are appropriate. The support team wonders how best to help him understand that instructional strategies that are necessary to help Samuel succeed.

It Works?

Mr. Simms could not believe that he was now thinking that the packaged reading program he had been using all year appeared to be working. He had fought its use because it was packaged and did not seem to allow for individualization. He wasn't sure what to do now that he had data showing that the students were making progress.

137
....

APPENDIX C
Annotated
Vignette
Summaries

What Was She Thinking?

Mrs. Hanks remembered thinking last spring that she was so lucky to finally have a special education support person assigned for the new school year to create materials for the children with disabilities included in her fifth-grade classroom. Now that the teacher had dropped off the box of supplies she had created for her students, Mrs. Hanks wondered how would these help? The teacher had not consulted with her in terms of the curriculum she used, the needs of the students, her teaching style, or any of the other things she thought should be considered when supporting the students included in her class.

Learning Environments and Social Interactions

Did Katie Receive a Fair Chance?

Mrs. Kell learns that she will be getting a new student. The student, Katie, had experienced behavior problems in her inclusive classroom and so was being placed in a self-contained special education class with a label of emotional disturbance. When Mrs. Kell reviews the records, she finds no evidence of positive behavior support planning for Katie in her inclusive placements, and wonders if Katie was really given a fair chance to achieve in that placement.

What's an Aide to Do?

When Felicia throws a book at another student, her aide, Ms. Wang, is surprised. When the teacher appears annoyed, Ms. Wang isn't sure what to do. She feels that no one has helped her learn how to predict Felicia's outbursts or how to modify instruction for Felicia.

How Does Ned Fit In?

Mrs. Kimura is asked to observe a student that the school district wants placed into her self-contained special education class. She goes to the student's inclusive placement in a first-grade class and feels that he could be successful there if he was given appropriate supports. She tells the school team this and suggests a positive behavior support plan be developed, but the first-grade teacher says she just wants him moved out of her class.

138
....

APPENDIX C

*Annotated
Vignette
Summaries*

How Far Can an Aide Go?

Mrs. Rajoub, the aide, has difficulty implementing the structured positive behavior support plan for her student, Kim. She also complains about the teacher to Kim's family. The teacher is frustrated because she is trying to build a relationship with the family and help with Kim's behavior, but Mrs. Rajoub is not helping in either area.

Study Skills or Homework?

Mrs. Graves found that her study skills class ended up being a time for her special education students to finish the homework from their other general education classes. She spent a lot of time organizing their work and helping them plan for the many classes they had. She felt this was important, but she also wanted to take some time to teach the students general study skills. She developed a plan to teach study skills one day a week, which meant she could continue with the homework activities on the other days.

Going around in Circles

Tom's aggressiveness continues to escalate and his teacher struggles with how to respond. The team agrees that a medical evaluation might prove helpful, but the parents' don't have insurance, and efforts to obtain an evaluation through other means have not proven successful. When Tom is finally referred to home teaching, his teacher wonders what else she could have done to help with Tom's behavioral issues.

Michael Deserves a Chance

Mrs. Skelton was called to help another special education teacher who was struggling with a student. She gives suggestions and even works with a district specialist the help the teacher. The teacher seems receptive but doesn't ever seem to implement the suggestions she is given. The student's behavior continues to escalate, and the principal even says that he may call the police the next time the student gets aggressive.

Stop Teasing Me

Other kids know that Ricky gets upset if they say bad things about his mother, and so they often make insulting remarks just to see him get upset. This mostly happens at recess but the problems carry over into the classroom.

Language

Can I Do It?

Mr. T. was excited about trying out the sheltered instruction strategies he had just learned. He thought this might just be the ticket to helping him meet his students' language development needs as well as their individual learning needs.

Whose Language Barrier?

Ms. Cox struggles with feelings of guilt over not being fluent in Spanish so that she can talk directly with her students' families. She'd like to be able to speak with all of her students' families but since there were families who also spoke Tagalog and Farsi, she wasn't sure how she could ever resolve this guilt.

Bridging Language barriers

Jazmine's school support team worked with her family to provide an appropriate education with special attention to Jazmine's hearing impairment. When the family finally agrees to use an FM device to help Jazmine hear her teacher, the family asks why this hadn't been suggested earlier. Since the team had suggested it, they began to examine what had happened with translation at earlier meetings.

What Have I Gotten Myself Into?

Mr. Folger switched from teaching sixth through eighth grades to teaching fourth and fifth grades. He is happy about the change but is unsure of how to proceed when the principal asks him to teach an English language development class. He is willing to try but feels uncertain about how to best proceed.

Labeling Dilemma

When Diana makes great progress with her speech and language therapy, her IEP team is unsure about how to ensure that Diana obtains the support she needs when her label no longer fits her situation.

"Toilet, Water Closet, Bano . . ."

Ms. Ahmadinejad is embarrassed once again as she has misunderstood what Oscar was trying to tell her. She has interpreted Oscar's behavior as noncompliance when he was just trying to tell her something but didn't have the words to do so. She is convinced that she needs to help Oscar find a way to communicate his needs so they can both understand each other.

Twin Talk

Ahmed and Ara are identical twins who have significant language delays. Both boys have articulation problems, which have impaired their ability to develop distinguishable oral language. As a result, their communication skills between peers has been hampered. Also, they use "twin talk" that is unintelligible to others and further delays the development of useful oral language.

Who Speaks for Joey?

Joey is a fifth-grade student who receives special services because of a speech and language impairment. Although Joey is able to speak English well, his teacher thinks he is in a state of learned helplessness. He thinks throughout Joey's life, family and friends have spoken for Joey, causing him to rely on others for communication.

Lost in Translation

Mr. Martin was having trouble communicating with Mahmoud and his family. The prereferral team at the school doesn't seem to understand the student's needs. He didn't know how to help them all see that Mahmoud's academic delays were making it difficult for him to participate in the general education classroom. Mr. Martin is frustrated by the lack of communication.

Instructional Planning

No Supplies for Mr. Kennedy

A week prior to the school year, Mr. Kennedy learns that he is being reassigned from his fourth- and fifth-grade class to a kindergarten/first-grade class. When he arrives, he finds that he has few supplies. The principal thinks that Mr. Kennedy's students won't understand the core curriculum materials, so he won't be getting any of those. Is he going to have to make up his own curriculum?

This Could Work

Mrs. Banks was nervous and excited. She had finally figured out how to match her students up with the general education teachers at her school for the new inclusion program she had developed. She matched teachers with students, based on their teaching/learning styles and specific characteristics. Mrs. Banks put a lot of time and effort into this planning, and now hopes the school team will accept her suggestions.

Planning for Mark

The co-teaching relationship between Kelly and Linda seems to be going well. They are using a tool called the Planning Pyramid. As they progress in their planning practices, the two teachers begin to wonder if there is something missing in their planning process.

I Did It!

Mrs. Maldern sat back and thought, "I did it!" She had completed assessment of all her students in reading and math and created small groups based on their ability levels. Although the small groups helped target individual needs, there were still many individual needs set forth in each child's IEP. After creating a cross-matrix of every student's goals, she was able to plan lessons that targeted goals that were closely related. She felt now that instruction would be more effective and help her with her utilize time management.

How Will I Do It?

Mr. Ecks wondered how he would ever support all his students. He had 30 students on his caseload and had to figure out how to provide them with support in all of their general education high school classes. How could he be in so many different places at the same time?

Is This Okay?

Mrs. Smith was worried about putting five of her special education students in the same general education class, but she knew that if she clustered them, then she could provide more direct support to them in their general education classes. Would the benefits outweigh the limitations of clustering?

How Many Grade Levels?

Mrs. Garza was interested in using the *Open Court* reading program that her district just adopted but wasn't sure how to plan her day to cover the three different grade levels of students she had in her special education classroom.

Teaching Addition

It was math time again and Mr. Peck wasn't sure at all about how well his planning would work out. He couldn't figure out how best to differentiate instruction so that some of his students could work on adding two-digit sums and others could work on basic number identification.

Assessment

How to Test?

Jason was required to take a formal standardized test for his triennial but he became very upset when the testing began. His teacher figured out a way to give him the test in a more informal setting but worried that this might invalidate the scoring.

Are You Sure?

Mrs. Freeman had to laugh when she saw LaDawn and the new school psychologist return to her class. She had warned the psychologist about taking LaDawn out of her familiar environment for testing, as LaDawn didn't handle changes in her routine well. Mrs. Freeman now wondered how they would test LaDawn as required by the district.

Finding a Way

When the district mandates benchmark assessments for all students, Ms. Bedard finds it difficult to test all of her students. Since most are still developing oral language, a score in phonemic awareness and running records are not always an accurate measure of the students' abilities. With the use of modifications, Ms. Bedard must find alternative ways to assess her students that will reflect their true levels of performance.

Going through the Motions

At Omar's IEP meeting, his teacher, Mrs. Michaels, is surprised when parts of the IEP document are skipped over by other members of the team and when objectives are written that don't really fit with the assessments that Mrs. Michaels prepared so carefully. She isn't sure how to deal with the team just "going through the motions."

Meaningful Monitoring

Mr. Lind helped his students develop great portfolios with artifacts from their class work but found that these didn't really help him write his IEPs. He wondered about how to develop a monitoring system that would provide him with needed information for developing IEPs.

How Much Can I Do?

Mrs. Dean was happy that she finally had instructions on how to perform the legally required alternate testing for her students with significant disabilities.

However, when she saw that it would take many hours to test each student, she wondered how she would ever do this.

Too Much Already!

Mr. Kane cringed when the Discrete Trial Therapy support provider arrived in his classroom. He knew that he would be asked for the data sheets that he was required to fill out but also knew that he would have to explain why the intense data collection was hard to accomplish with all the other duties he had to perform.

Am I Cheating?

Mrs. Thalia knew she was doing the right thing but also knew others would think she was cheating. She was tired of her students not performing well on their benchmark assessments, so she had started to teach them the key terminology that she knew would be on those assessments.

Professionalism and Ethical Practices

What Do I Ask For?

Mr. Mason is in his first year of teaching and keeps asking for support with mixed outcomes. He is worried that he'll get in trouble for asking for too much help or that he won't know what to ask for when help is offered.

Where Is She?

For two years, Mrs. Jones has been working with the same program specialist— the person designated to act between class/school site and district office. Although she realizes that the program specialist's responsibilities are numerous, Mrs. Jones's patience has been tested due to difficulties in reaching the program specialist when important issues arise. Also, return phone calls are rarely returned to Mrs. Jones, making her feel like her issues and/or students may not take precedence over another school site. Where should she go for help?

Why Isn't Your Homework Done?

Paul has muscular dystrophy and his health has begun to deteriorate. His parents don't think that homework is the most important way for him to spend the limited time he has left. Students in his class earn an off-campus lunch if they do 95 percent of their homework, and so now Paul's doing his homework. His teacher wonders if motivating students this way is the right thing to do.

Setting Limits?

Ms. Low is committed to doing all she can to help her students learn and stay in school but all her colleagues tell her that she needs to set limits. Home visits and staying late after school are just too much, they say.

The Loss of a Talented Teacher

Mr. Lavine taught kindergarten for eight years and saw the standards for his students change over the years. He found there was less time to spend on creative and exploratory projects and learning through play. He finally felt that he couldn't keep doing what he was being asked to do and so thought of leaving the profession all together.

A New System

Mrs. Davis has tried to meet Nick's needs within her classroom but keeps feeling like he just doesn't fit in. She feels that her class may not be the most appropriate placement for Nick but isn't sure how to raise these concerns at the IEP meeting so they can be addressed in a professional manner.

Should I Ask for Help?

Miss Webb is a new teacher and is being particularly challenged by one of her students, Jack. She feels she needs help but thinks that if she asks for help too soon, the principal and school district administration will think she is not a good teacher.

Paperwork Overload

Maya received an F in history and her parents now want to know if she received all of the accommodations and modifications that were listed on her IEP. Her resource teacher tells the parents that she did receive all the accommodations and modifications in the general education classroom, but that there is no documentation for this.

Why Are You Teaching?

In order to complete a college assignment, Debbie observed Mrs. Martin's classroom. Debbie was taken aback by the disorganized and drab classroom. It appeared to Debbie that the students were not being motivated to learn and that minimal teaching was taking place. Debbie wondered why Mrs. Martin was teaching.

Collaboration

No Time to Eat

Two teachers wonder if they will ever have time to eat lunch. Although both have enjoyed the benefits of their co-teaching relationship, their collaborative planning lunches are becoming more and more complicated. The two teachers are becoming frustrated by these challenges.

Homework

Jeff's homework always came back incomplete or incorrect, which upset his teacher. His parents felt it was important for Jeff to do the homework on his own, since it was the school's job to teach those skills. His teacher really wants the parents to help Jeff with his homework but isn't sure how to handle their response.

Get to Work!

Mrs. Chapman's classroom aides continually socialize during the day rather than perform their work duties. Although they have all discussed this frequently and developed plans to change, the problems still continue. Mrs. Chapman thought she had done what needed to be done to pull together a strong instructional team to help teach all her students, but she now questions herself.

Let the Teacher Teach

Noel's parents give her teacher multiple demands for therapy and structured discrete trial instruction, which make it difficult for her teacher to figure out how to meet all of Noel's needs as well as the needs of the other students.

The Ties that Bind . . .

Henry's transition to Mrs. Moore's classroom did not go as smoothly as everyone hoped. After making great strides in the primary classroom, his transition led to behavior problems and resistance to learning. His new teacher was also resistant to receiving help from the primary-grade teacher who knew Henry well. When she learns that Henry is being transferred, she is upset because she wonders what she could have done to help in this situation.

What More Can I Do?

Mr. Strode tried to work with Kayleigh's family but was frequently frustrated when they didn't follow through on plans or attend meetings. The family's social worker was supposed to help with this but the social worker also didn't attend

146

....

APPENDIX C

Annotated
Vignette
Summaries

meetings. He was tired of all this and wondered what more he could do to work with the family and the social worker.

Mrs. Who?

Dr. Janks was interested in visiting a new teacher he was charged with assessing in terms of how well the teacher was implementing instruction that fit the state standards for teachers. When he arrived at the school site, he followed instructions that all visitors should go to the school office first. He was then surprised when the office staff didn't recognize the name of the special education teacher or seem to know where the class was located. What does this say about the school and its approach to including students with disabilities?

Can I Change Mrs. Asper?

Mrs. Hill had trouble managing her classroom aide, Mrs. Asper, and although she tried everything she could think of to help her aide perform her duties, Mrs. Asper continued to be absent frequently and not to follow through on the instructional plans that Mrs. Hill developed. Mrs. Hill wondered if she could ever change Mrs. Asper and help her to contribute effectively to the classroom routine.

Bibliography

Coots, J. J., Bishop, K. D., & Grenot-Scheyer, M. (1998). Supporting elementary age students with significant disabilities in general education classrooms: What teachers say and do. *Education and Training in Mental Retardation and Developmental Disabilities, 33* (4), 317–330.

Council for Exceptional Children. (2003). *What every special educator must know: Ethics, standards, and guidelines for special educators* (5th ed.). Upper Saddle River, NJ: Pearson, Merrill Prentice Hall.

Eby, J. W., Herrell, A. L., & Hicks, J. (2002). *Reflective planning, teaching, and evaluation: K–12.* Upper Saddle River, NJ: Merrill Prentice Hall.

Grenot-Scheyer, M., Fisher, M., & Staub, D. (2001). *At the end of the day: Lessons learned in inclusive education.* Baltimore, MD: Brookes.

Henderson, J. (2001). *Reflective teaching: Professional artistry through inquiry.* Upper Saddle River, NJ: Merrill Prentice Hall.

Reagan, T. G., Case, C. W., & Brubacher, J. W. (2000). *Becoming a reflective educator: How to build a culture of inquiry in the schools* (2nd ed.). Thousand Oaks, CA: Corwin.

Riehl, C. J. (2000). The principal's role in creating inclusive schools for diverse students: A review of normative, empirical, and critical literature on the practice of educational administration. *Review of Educational Research, 70* (1), 55–81.

Schumm, J. S., Vaughn, S., & Harris, J. (1997). Pyramid power for collaborative planning. *Teaching Exceptional Children, 29,* 62–66.

Wilson, S. M., & Berne, J. (1999). Teacher learning and the acquisition of professional knowledge: An examination of research on contemporary professional development, *Review of Research in Education, 24,* 173–209.

York-Barr, J., Sommers, W. A., Ghere, G. S., & Montie, J. (2001). *Reflective practice to improve schools: An action guide for educators.* Thousand Oaks, CA: Corwin.

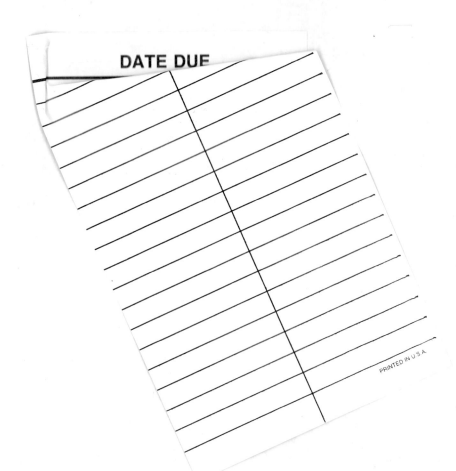

DATE DUE

PRINTED IN U.S.A.